Wool Rug Hooking

Tara Darr

©2005 Tara Darr
Published by

kp books
An Imprint of F+W Publications

700 East State Street • Iola, WI 54990-0001
715-445-2214 • 888-457-2873

Library of Congress Catalog Number: 2004098437
ISBN: 0-87349-893-3

Edited by Maria L. Turner
Designed by Kara Grundman
Printed in the United States of America

Introduction

So many times over the past several years I have been asked the question, "What is rug hooking?" The best possible answer I can give is, "Let me show you!"

Rug hooking has become a great passion of mine and has provided me with an outlet for the challenges of day-to-day life. With every loop I've ever hooked, there is a story behind the wool or the design and I wish to share some of these thoughts with you throughout these pages.

I encourage you to be creative and develop your own hooking style. Nothing about rug hooking is set in stone. Change the rules every now and then to fit your needs.

Rug hooking is exhilarating, and I wish you much joy and success as you express yourself through your hooking projects. To truly enjoy your art, you must love what you are doing and be passionate about it. I challenge you to explore rug hooking with open eyes and a creative heart. Happy hookin'!

Table of Contents

Chapter 6

Projects   **64**

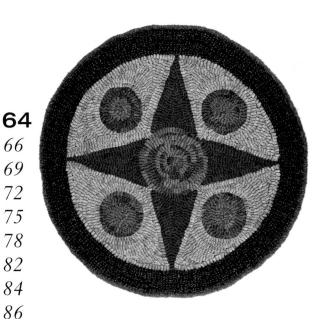

Resources   128

Chapter 1

Age-Old Craft

Rug hooking is an age-old craft that evolved out of necessity. The exact origin of rug hooking depends on whom you speak with or what you read. We do know that this wonderfully historic craft has come a long way since the days of long ago.

Origin

The exact location or time that rug hooking originated is not known and is quite controversial. Some suggest that immigrants from England, Scandinavia and Scotland brought the first resemblances of hooked rugs into the Americas. There are other theories that indicate the craft originated in Egypt between the third and seventh centuries. While still others insist rug hooking began in China or Europe.

From my research and study of hooked rugs, and the beliefs of many rug-hooking historians, it seems most logical that immigrants brought rug hooking to the colonies.

Photo by Jodi H. Beyeler and courtesy Goshen College, 2004.

This wool on burlap rug found in Lancaster County, Pa., dates back to the 1870s, by which time the making of hooked rugs had spread westward from New England. It is from the Maija Walters collection.

Old Mennonite pictorial rugs, like this one called Winter Sled Ride (circa 1950), often depicted horses, which reflected their rural setting and occupations. This particular rug from Ontario, Canada, is made of mixed cloths on burlap and came from the collection of Phyllis and Ervin Beck.

Edna Shantz of Ontario, Canada, who designed this wool and burlap rug in 1932, dyed the colors used in the flowers and hooked it on a quilt frame for use on the floor of the parlor of her parents' home. It is quite an elaborate example for a piece of that time period when so many were struggling through the Great Depression.

This rug, made between 1930 and 1940 of wool on burlap, depicts the common use of garden florals in early designs. It is from the collection of Phyllis and Ervin Beck and believed to have come from Lancaster County, Pa.

It is clear that rug hooking came about out of necessity to warm homes in the early to mid-1800s. It appears that rug hooking originated here in America in the northern colonies during that time frame, but there is also documented evidence of hooked rugs in the maritime provinces of Canada around the same time. Early hooked rugs were hooked on coffee, grain and sugar feed sacks because burlap was not yet available. Worn-out clothing was thriftily recycled into these imaginative rugs of the past that were created to warm the hearth. Rug hooking spread quickly as this age-old craft became known.

The seamen of that era enjoyed the craft of rug hooking while passing the time alone or with their wives. It is said that these sailors would fashion hooks from nails on sticks. These rugs were of simple, innocent designs depicting nautical and geometric images and were hooked on foundations of canvas cloth using strands of yarn or rope.

The rug hookers of long ago were not inhibited as we are today by perfection. Instead, people drew their hooking patterns from the heart and often created some rather whimsical images. The first hooked rugs can easily be considered pure primitive art. Often, shapes and images were drawn misshapen and out of proportion: houses that are larger than 1,000-year-old trees; children larger than life; birds larger than trees; large, misshapen flowers and so forth. Normally, the drawn images located centrally in the rugs were the "important" objects

in the artists' lives or something of meaning.

Common objects in rug hooking were quite diversified. Special moments or familiar objects, such as home, pets, children and gardens can be seen in many early rugs. Not all hooked rugs reveal peaceful, calming moments. In fact, some rugs have brought forth startling revelations depicting bitter feuds and unhappy moments in the hooker's past.

Hooked rugs in beginning America served the main purpose of providing warmth on the floors (which at that time were dirt) and to keep drafts from the doorways. In the 1800s, the women of the households were the creators and were mainly among the rural and urban middle class. As rug hooking evolved, they were more objects

This wool on burlap rug was created circa 1940 by sisters Mabel Erb Kauffman and Anna Erb King of Hesston, Kan., during a time when rug hooking was near its peak, as the United States was about to enter World War II. It came from the collection of Dan Kauffman, Mabel's son.

Made between 1940 and 1950, this rug by Mrs. Hoover and her daughter of Waterloo, Ontario, shows just how clever rug hookers could be. The mother-daughter duo used shoelaces (the cloth with metallic threads), a polyester binding (to mend the frayed edges) and a sewn-on fringe that was an unusual addition to a hooked rug. It is from the Phyllis and Ervin Beck collection.

After World War II, rug-hooking interest declined, but some nice examples can still be found, like this piece made circa 1950 in Ontario, Canada. It is from the collection of Phyllis and Ervin Beck.

This wool on burlap rug, which was hooked by Pennsylvanian Mary Umberger circa 1970, shows a design more often found in quilts than in hooked rugs. The use of colors creates an effect similar to that of "flame" embroidery and the look follows the flavor of art in the late-'60s through 1970s. It is from the collection of Liz and Ralph Hernley.

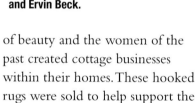

of beauty and the women of the past created cottage businesses within their homes. These hooked rugs were sold to help support the households.

Around the 1850s Edward Sands Frost, a peddler from Biddeford, Maine, and a Civil War Yankee veteran, created a hook for his own wife to make hooked rugs. While at home, retired because of ill health, he watched his wife draw crude images to hook and the spark was ignited to improve hooking. From there his ingenious mind went on to create tin stencil designs that could be stamped onto feed sacks. Frost's simple idea helped raise the rug-hooking standard, marked the beginning of simple, uninhibited creativity in rug hooking and brought forth mass production in the craft. Frost found no one brave

enough to invest in his idea, so he sold his early stamped designs from his peddler's cart, saving money all the while to further his business of selling printed patterns. Rug hooking spread, but the need for one's own creativity decreased.

Ralph Burnham, another New Englander, continued the mass production approach to rug hooking by reproducing and selling more patterns in the early 20th century. He also repaired old hooked rugs.

After the Civil War, the art of rug hooking began to fade and was not revived again until after World War I, more than 50 years later. During the Depression of the 1930s, people turned to rug making once again and the craft hit its highest interest during World War II. In times of great despair and hostility, rug

hooking allowed people to create a comfort zone and release for creativity in men and women alike.

After World War II, interest in rug hooking declined, as tastes seemed to change. Linoleum, tiles and wall-to-wall carpets slowly evolved and hooked rugs went to the wayside. Women began to work outside the home and had little time for hobbies.

Today, history is repeating itself once again. A renewed interest in this wonderful craft has come to the forefront recently. The need to create and calm the soul through rug hooking provides a release from day-to-day reality. Create your own piece of history for your family, one that will extend on into the future and show this new era in rug making history.

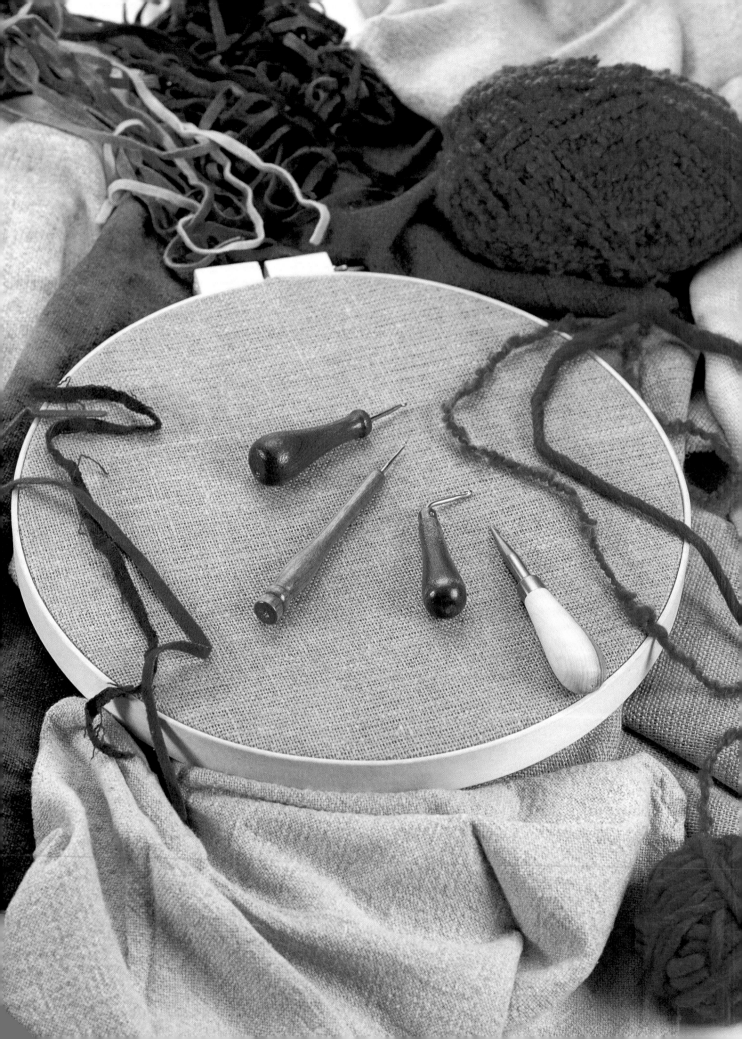

Chapter 2

Tools and Supplies

Gather your supplies and enjoy the warm, relaxing world of rug hooking. With only a few minor items to start with, you can be on your way to creating a cherished heirloom.

Foundation Fabric

Foundation fabric is of great importance to any rug-hooking project. This will be the fabric you pull your loops of wool through to create your rug. A good-quality, strong backing that will last a lifetime is important to any rug hooker. The most commonly used fabrics on the market today are burlap, monk's cloth, rug warp, loosely woven wool and linen.

Look for foundation fabrics with a density 10 to 12 epi (ends per inch) if you enjoy the type of rugs that appear in this book, all of which were hooked on linen.

To find the epi, lay the cloth on a flat work surface, place a ruler on it and count the number of threads in an inch. The higher the number, the tighter the weave; such tighter weaves are better fabric for "fine" cuts of wool. The lower the number, the looser the weave; such fabrics will be more forgiving for primitive or wider cuts.

Try different types of rug-hooking foundation fabrics. Use what you like and can afford, and your projects will turn out wonderfully.

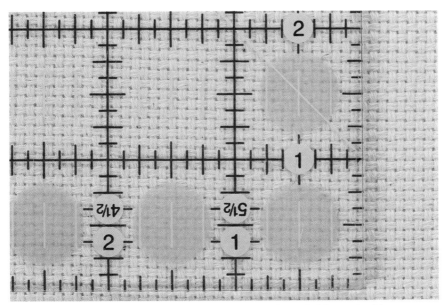

The fabric shown here is the proper type of monk's cloth needed for rug hooking. Monk's cloth that is intended for rug hooking should have an average of 10 to 12 epi or "ends per inch."

Burlap

Burlap is a good strong foundation that is made from jute and is very inexpensive. Unfortunately, it is very rough in texture and is more fragile.

There are two main types of burlap: standard or primitive burlap, which is used for wider cuts of wool and has a looser weave, and Scottish burlap, which is slightly heavier and is more evenly woven. Burlap is available in 48" and 60" widths. Do not hook on the commonly found burlap in crafting stores; it is not evenly woven and the fibers used to make the fabric are short and fall apart easily.

Many new rug hookers begin hooking on primitive or Scottish burlap to keep beginning costs minimal. Burlap can be used to hook medium width cuts up to primitive wider cuts of wool. Since burlap is stiff, it can be tough to pull extremely wide widths of wool, such as ½" strips, through the tougher fibers.

You may see old rugs that are deteriorating as the burlap wastes away. Today's burlap is substantially better, but over time, it too will deteriorate if not taken care of properly. Rugs made on burlap should not be subjected to water or continually exposed to heat or sunlight. Water will promote the rotting process in the burlap fibers, and heat or sun will only help break

down the fibers more quickly.

Many historic rugs from 50 to 100 years old are still intact today and were hooked on burlap, so don't think hooking on burlap is a bad thing. The rug will not "disappear" in a few years. But if you intend to make projects that will last for a couple hundred years, you might consider using something other than burlap.

Monk's Cloth

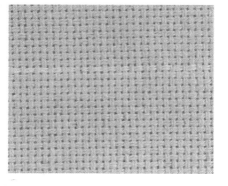

Monk's cloth is an evenly woven, two-ply, 100 percent cotton fabric. Because cotton is the most elastic of plant fibers, monk's cloth is flexible, medium in weight and easy to hook in. Hook fine cuts up to wider primitive cuts on monk's cloth.

Monk's cloth was one of the first commercially manufactured fabrics and has been in use for more than 60 years. It is the most commonly chosen fabric amongst rug hookers and is the easiest to find. Use rug hooking monk's cloth, called 2x2 grade or with 10 to 12 epi (see sidebar), and not the common 5 epi variety found in crafts stores for crocheting and stitching purposes.

Monk's cloth is better at resisting water damage than burlap. Some experts say it is washable, but fibers can still break down after being repeatedly subjected to water.

Monk's cloth also does not "shed" fibers in the fabric. Burlap and some types of linen (mainly a stiffer primitive brand) have small "hairs" on the fabric, which tend to make their way to the tops of your finished hooked rugs and end up needing to be trimmed off.

For larger rugs and hall runners, monk's cloth is a wonderful choice, as it is available in 244"-wide pieces and smaller 60"-wide cuts.

One downside to this type of cloth is that it stretches more. If the fabric is stretched too tightly in a frame or hoop, it will lose its shape, the design will become contorted and a rippling effect occurs on the finished rug.

Because monk's cloth is also very soft and has more weave, hooking extremely wide widths is more challenging. Try hooking an eight-cut (¼" wide) or less in monk's cloth.

Rug Warp

Rug warp, also known as warp cloth, is best for finer cuts of wool and is the "sturdier" cousin of monk's cloth. It is woven of heavier gauge cotton fibers, which stretch less but are coarser. Such coarseness makes rug warp tougher to hook on and harder on your hands.

Rug warp is not the most favored choice of backings between rug hookers, but there are several qualities to consider. It is evenly woven and great for finer cuts, but to hook a "primitive" style that uses wider wool strips, like the designs in this book, rug warp will prove challenging.

Because rug warp is heavier in weight, it is a better choice for smaller projects.

Linen

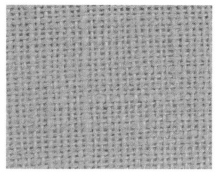

Linen is the most expensive foundation to hook on, but it has many benefits. Grown from the flax plant, it is one of the oldest fibers known to man.

Linen has better strength than cotton or jute (burlap) and is the most stabile fabric for hooking, as it will not shrink. It is easy to hook on and is good for fine cuts up to the widest of primitive cuts of wool. Linen is easier to hook many different widths in one project without distorting the actual rug itself when finishing. Linen is a very forgiving fabric and will easily go back into place if you need to pull your strips of wool out and re-hook an area. Hooking a ½"-wide strip of wool on linen is like pulling wool through butter when using the right type of hook. (See page 18 for hook information.)

Linen is also the most durable rug-hooking foundation fabric. It has been proven not to deteriorate and will outlast cotton and burlap. It is said to be a washable fabric, but the cautious prefer dry cleaning.

There are many different types of linen, from stiff to soft and silky. Linen also comes in many "natural"-colored shades.

Tara's Tip: *Linen by far is my chosen hooking fabric. I use a soft linen and rarely use any other fabric. My hooking is more efficient and I have less of a struggle hooking larger widths.*

Loosely Woven Wool

A growing trend today is hooking on loosely woven 100 percent wool. If you come across wool that is just too loose in weave to hook with, simply use it as a foundation fabric instead.

By hooking on wool, you often can eliminate hooking the entire background of the project. Choose a brilliant blue to hook a bright sun or floating flowers. Hook your favorite dog on a great plaid wool.

Keep the wool taut in your hoop or frame and try to minimize stretching the fabric. Wool will bounce back into shape as long as it's properly cared for. When stretching the wool onto your gripper frame or in your hoop, remember not to overstretch it. The fabric should be flat and not drooping down inside the frame, so it is easier to hook on.

Do not pack your loops, especially when hooking on wool, as the wool will pucker or ripple and no attempt to keep it flat will work.

Frames

A variety of rug hooking hoops and frames are available today. Each has its own benefits. Choosing the right frame can mean a world of difference in your hooking. The key is to try as many different types of frames as you can before investing in one.

Hoops

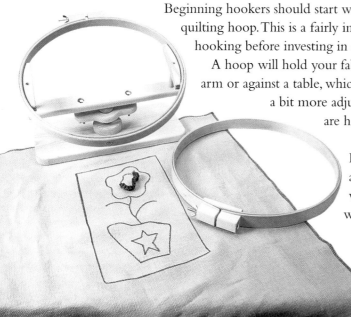

Beginning hookers should start with a simple, strong 1"-wide, 14"-diameter good-quality quilting hoop. This is a fairly inexpensive investment that will give you a taste of rug hooking before investing in a more expensive frame.

A hoop will hold your fabric taut. It can be adjusted in your lap, the crook of your arm or against a table, which will free up your hands for hooking. A hoop does take a bit more adjustment with your hands and arms to manage it while you are hooking.

A favorite hoop among many rug hookers is the Gruber Lap Hoop (see Resources, page 128). This frame is on a wood base that rests on your lap and swivels. Working with this frame easily allows you to work with both hands, without having to try to balance a regular quilting hoop.

Tara's Tip: If you prefer hooking on a hoop, you may want to invest in a longer bolt and wing nut for the top of your hoop. As you progress to larger rugs and you have more bulk being sandwiched between the hoops, you will find that the standard bolt on quilting frames isn't long enough. A trip to the local hardware store will solve this problem easily.

The Gruber hoop lap frame and a standard quilting hoop.

Gripper Frames

There are many "gripper" type frames available today, with more always advancing the last. Some personal favorites are detailed here. Each frame has its own individual benefits, but each frame holds the foundation fabrics extremely well.

Check the Resources list on page 128 for several other frame suppliers that aren't shown here. Shop around and ask many questions before investing in a frame, as they are more costly than a standard hoop, but well worth the investment.

There are several gripper frames on the market today. Gripper frames hold your foundation fabric very well, allowing you to hook with ease.

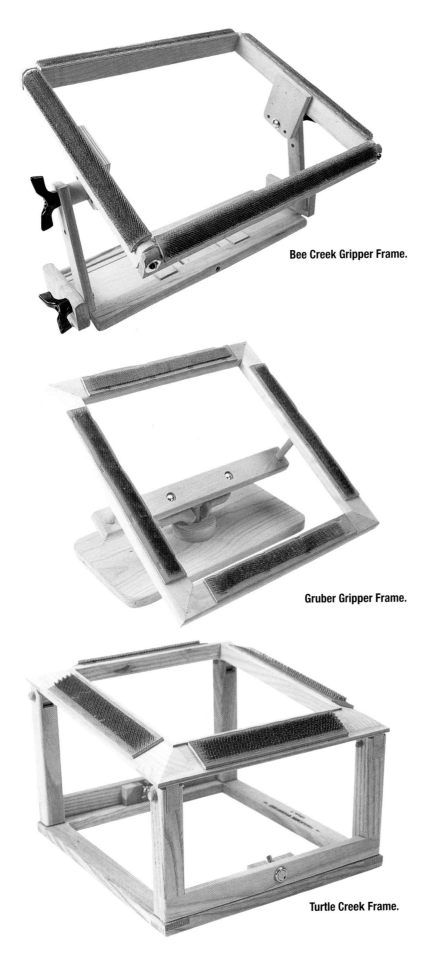

Bee Creek Gripper Frame

This handmade wood frame is completely collapsible, which is a nice feature when traveling or storing the frame. One of the best features of this frame is that the gripper strips (the sharp metal teeth-like strips that run around the edges of the frame) meet in the corners, which allows you to hook further into the corners of your project before moving. The height is adjustable to many different levels from collapsed and flat for travel and up to 10" high in use. This frame also tilts forward and back and rests easily on your lap or on a table.

Bee Creek Gripper Frame.

Gruber Gripper Frame

The Gruber Gripper Frame is an excellent midsize frame choice. It is 14" square and has 10" of gripper strips on each side. This frame also swivels 360 degrees, which allows easy access to the entire hooking project. It is easy to assemble and is a convenient size for traveling. This handmade frame is mounted on a ball joint system, so the entire frame can be adjusted in many different directions. The ball joint allows you to hook in different directions without constantly moving your pattern from place to place; you can simply adjust the frame to the direction that best suits your needs.

Gruber Gripper Frame.

Turtle Creek Frame

The Turtle Creek Frame comes in two different sizes. The frame in the photo, which is the smaller version, is 10" x 11". There is also a larger frame that is available, which is 13½" x 16". It is a great beginner frame and an excellent choice for traveling. Handmade in Ohio, this frame is distributed through Kindred Spirits (Resources, page 128).

Turtle Creek Frame.

Wool Cutters

There are several ways to cut your wool fabric into strips for rug hooking. Many people prefer to cut by hand, while others enjoy the convenience of a cloth "stripper" machine.

Ripping wool that is approximately ½" to ⅝" wide on-grain.

Cutting a ½"- to ⅝"-wide strip of wool in half that has been previously ripped on-grain.

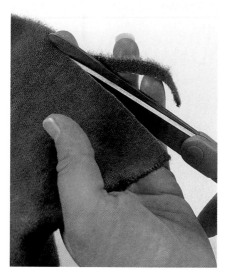

Cutting a piece of wool into a ¼"- to ⅜"-wide strip using scissors.

By Hand

Most people begin to cut the strips necessary for hooking in one of two ways.

The first option is to rip the wool on-grain into ½" to ⅝" strips along the width and then cut the strip in half with a pair of scissors, as shown in the accompanying photos here.

The second is to cut ¼" or ⅜" strips along the width of the whole using a sharp pair of scissors.

Both methods work well and look wonderful in primitive-style rugs, as the strips tend to be a little uneven.

Rotary Cutter and Mat

You may cut wool strips using a rotary cutter, ruler and quilting mat. This method of cutting strips proves slightly more difficult, but can be done with practice. The wool has a tendency to slide easily under your ruler while cutting, making cutting off-grain a problem. Prevent slippage by holding the ruler down with firm pressure and have your wool lying straight under the ruler.

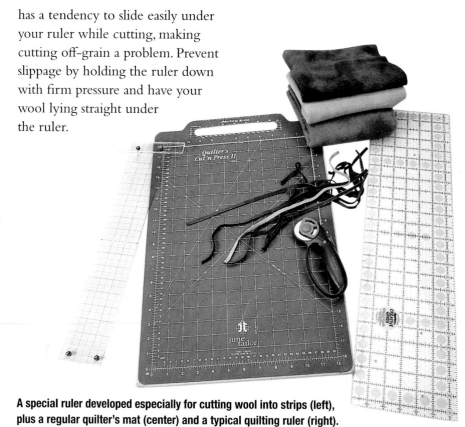

A special ruler developed especially for cutting wool into strips (left), plus a regular quilter's mat (center) and a typical quilting ruler (right).

Mechanical Cutters

In time, you may choose to invest in a cloth-stripping machine like the one shown here. These strippers are timesaving machines that cut with great efficiency. There are currently three companies in the United States that produce strippers, as well as one in Canada.

One such U.S. manufacturer is the Fraser Company, which makes the Bliss and the Fraser cutters. The Bliss has suction feet, which help to keep the machine in place while cutting on your tabletop. The Fraser model is a clamp-type cutter, provides a sturdier cutting action and has an adjustable side guide for wide strips. The Bliss and Fraser both have screw-on cutter heads that are easy to change with the handy tool included with the cutter.

Another U.S. machine is the Rigby. The Rigby is also a clamp-on machine and some models even have a two-cutter head feature, making it easier to cut more strips at the same time.

The newest cutter manufactured in the U.S. is the Townsend. This cutter uses the latest technology to allow smooth cutting of woolen fabrics. The Townsend cutter is compact, clamps down and has cutting heads that are easily changeable with just a "click."

Also available is the elite Bolivar cutter from Nova Scotia, Canada. The Bolivar uses a scissor-like action and has three blades that are permanently mounted. To change the blade for a different-sized cut, just change the housing.

Cutter Heads

With all cloth stripper machines, you need to make a decision on how wide your wool strips need to be. When working with wider widths of wool, such as #7 and above, you are working more in the "primitive" style of rug hooking. The projects in this book are primarily hooked in #8 and higher, using a #6 sparingly for details.

Cloth stripper machines that are available in today's market can cut strips from $\frac{1}{16}$" to $\frac{1}{2}$" wide. In hooker terms though, you would refer to strip sizes by saying, "I hook using a #6 or a #8 cut," with the six and eight designating the sizes of the cutter wheel.

Cutter Wheel Strip Sizes

#2 creates a $\frac{1}{16}$"-wide strip

#3 creates a $\frac{3}{32}$"-wide strip

#4 creates a $\frac{1}{8}$"-wide strip

#5 creates a $\frac{5}{32}$"-wide strip

#6 creates a $\frac{6}{32}$"-wide strip

#7 creates a $\frac{7}{32}$"-wide strip

#8 creates an $\frac{1}{4}$"-wide strip

#8.5 creates a $\frac{5}{16}$"-wide strip

#9 creates a $\frac{3}{8}$"-wide strip

#10 creates a $\frac{1}{2}$"-wide strip

Above, you will see the size cutter wheels available for cloth stripping machines today and their designated widths. Luckily, all cutters use the same standard numbers when referring to sizes of strips. Please note when comparing cutters that all cutters may not offer every size of cutter wheel that is standard on the market.

Several mechanical cutters, commonly known as "strippers" are available in today's rug hooking market.

Scissors and Tweezers

Choose the right scissors and tweezers and your project will move right along.

Any sharp pair of scissors will work, but scissors that are meant for appliqué-type work are ideal. A pair of bent shank scissors helps you direct the blades just where you want them to go with little effort or twisting of the wrist.

A simple pair of needle-nose tweezers prove a useful tool in rug hooking, as some foundation fabrics tend to be a little "hairy." And sometimes tweed, textured and more loosely woven wools will leave small wool fibers sticking up throughout your project.

Appliqué scissors, bent shank scissors and long tweezers.

Hooks

To begin rug hooking, choose a simple hook, and as you advance, find a hook that more suits your style of hooking and best fits your hand.

Ball-Type Hooks

One of the best hooks for a beginner is the ball-type hook. It's inexpensive and readily available. There are different hook sizes ranging from fine and medium to primitive. Ball hooks are generally small in size and fit most everyone's hand size. The ball hooks have a short shaft and fit into the palm of your hand.

Joan Moshimer ball hook and Fraser ball hook.

Specialty Hooks

There is a wide range of hooks beyond the basic ball hooks.

One favorite is the Hartman Ergo hook. It is designed with a small curve cutout of the wood handle to rest your thumb on, which relieves pressure to some points of your hand, allowing you to hook longer. The shanks on the Hartman hooks shown here are a big key to the benefits of this hook brand. The shank is pointy on the tip and gets wider as it meets the wooden shaft of the hook, which helps ease strain on your hand while hooking. The further the shaft is pushed into the rug-hooking foundation, the wider the opening will be, allowing you

to pull your strips of wool through with little effort. Try this hook when hooking #8 and wider cuts.

The Meno Trigger Grip hook was developed by a woman with multiple sclerosis, who still wanted to be able to hook. It is wonderful for people suffering from arthritis, carpal tunnel syndrome and multiple sclerosis. The hook is uniquely designed to allow several

different grip options and it works for either right- or left-handers.

The Miller Hook is a pencil-style hook that works well on a variety of foundation fabrics. It has a point on the tip, allowing it to enter the foundation fabric easily. This hook seems to work best with a #5 or #6 cut and on monk's cloth.

The Bent Shank Hook is designed to relieve stress on your hands and to help alleviate the problems related to arthritis and carpal tunnel. The shank portion of the hook is bent, allowing you to insert the hook into the foundation fabric without moving or twisting your wrist as much as you would with a traditional hook.

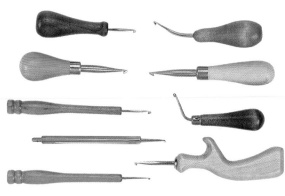

Several different types of hooks are available today, from top left down: Joan Moshimer Primitive Ball Hook; Hartman Primitive Ball Hook; Fraser Primitive Pencil Hook; Nancy Miller Primitive Pencil Hook; Fraser Fine Pencil Hook. From top right down are: the Burnham Bent Shank Hook; Hartman Primitive Ergo Hook; Joan Moshimer Primitive Bent Shank Hook; and a Meno Trigger Grip Hook.

Hooking Fabrics

Wool—100 percent wool—is the chosen fabric of most rug hookers, but the options do not end there. Several materials can be used for rug-hooking strips and all are readily available.

Keep in mind that a rug is only as good as the materials used to hook it. The rugs shown in this book all are made of 100 percent wools, but do not let this limit you. The type of hooking strips used depends on the projects and their end uses. Ask yourself as you are planning your rug: "Will this rug be a display piece hung on the wall or used on a table?" or "Will it be used as a floor rug?"

By answering these questions, you can easily determine whether to use purely wool or a mixture of fibers. Floor rugs should be hooked only in 100 percent wool or a very high blend of wool and other fiber. If you are framing your piece, creating a pillow or purse, or simply using the rug as a decorative tablemat, feel free to get creative and use other types of fibers in your rug hooking.

Durability is key. Your beautiful floor rug would have a limited life if you chose to hook it with 100 percent cotton homespun while it adorns a high-traffic area of your floor. Don't misunderstand: Homespun fabrics are great for

hooking strips because of the plaids that are available and the look they create when hooked, but do not trust them to hold up underfoot after repeated use over time.

Wool

Most rug hookers prefer 100 percent flannel or medium-weight wool for several reasons. Wool is a durable fabric that will last a lifetime if properly cared for, it is easy to hand-dye in your own home, and it is resistant to soiling.

Flannel weight wool is a tightly woven fabric that weighs between 11 and 13 ounces per yard. Look for 100 percent wool, but don't pass

Several different types of fabrics and fibers can be used for rug hooking.

up a blend that can be used "as is" and doesn't need to be dyed. The rug-hooking limit for such blends is 80 percent wool and 20 percent other synthetic fiber. The lesser the amount of wool, the more chances of unraveling in your work.

When you begin, use only 100 percent wool. Even 20 percent "other" in a blend fabric can unravel while hooking, which can be discouraging for new hookers. As you become more familiar with hooking, venture into blends, cutting the strips a little wider and taking care as you hook not to separate the fibers.

There are two great ways to test your wools to see if they are 100 percent pure wool or blends. The first and easiest test is to pull a few threads from the fabric and burn them with a match. Pull the fibers from both directions of the weave so that you have the "warp" thread and the "woof" thread. If the fibers smell like burning hair or feathers, it is wool. A synthetic thread will have no odor and cotton will burn very quickly with little to no odor. Or if the remains when rubbed between your fingers turn to soot, it is wool. If hard crystals form, it's a high-blend wool and should be disregarded for rug hooking.

The other way to test your fabrics is to pour about a cup of bleach into an old jar and toss in a 1" to 2" square of wool. If the fabric disappears, it's wool. If a few fibers remain, it is generally an 80/20 blend and would be safe to hook with. If many fibers remain, the wool content is too low and not good enough for hooking.

From time to time, you might try a thicker or "meatier" blanket weight wool. Blanket weight wool generally is between 14 and 16 ounces of weight per yard. It is a bit loftier and should be hooked using a primitive-style hook with a larger shank, like the Hartman Hook (see Resources, page 128). The larger shank on these hooks will create a larger opening on your rug hooking foundation, which will make it easier to pull loops through. It is also easiest to work with thicker woolens when hooking into a soft, flexible linen or monk's cloth foundation. Burlap cloth just does not have the extra "give" needed when hooking with thicker fibers; it can be done, but it is tougher on your hands. Hook blanket weight wools in #6 or #8 cut strips.

As you're out shopping or cruising the Internet, keep an open mind. Collect as many different wools as possible. Choose textures, plaids, solids, herringbones, checks, stripes, heathers, paisley patterns (often found in old woolen shawls), solids and even mohair. If you find a good price on a used garment or wool yardage, but just can't handle the color—buy it anyway. Wool often takes on a new look when hooked. Some plaids will take on a life of their own, picking up colors from the other wools surrounding them. And at other times, that hideous green your friend gave you might just be the spark you need in your next rug.

There are certain wools to stay away from when hooking because they are too stiff, too stretchy or too delicate and thin. Avoid all worsted weights, gabardines, melton, diagonally woven wool, jersey and serge woolens. Read the clothing tags or the fiber content on the end of bolt goods wisely. Use your best judgment.

For example, when you find the "perfect" men's jacket at a resale shop and the tag reads 100 percent wool, remember that most men's jackets on the market today are made from wool that is just too thin to hook with and are of worsted weight. Feel the fabric and really look at the garment before you purchase it. You'll get to know how good hooking wool feels and looks.

There are many sources for woolen fabrics. Browse the Internet, shop garage and rummage sales, visit your relatives' closets, ask friends for unwanted wool garments or go to the resale shops. Visit a rug-hooking shop, call some mail-order wool companies and ask for their wool mailers, or check into your local fabric or quilt shop. See Resources, page 128, for a place to start.

Mill-Dyed Wool

Mill-dyed wool is a phrase that can be a little confusing in the beginning. Mill-dyed wool is simply wool on the bolt that can be purchased by the yard and is dyed at the woolen mill instead of being hand-dyed. Mill-dyed wools come in a gorgeous array of colors, textures, plaids, herringbones and

Selection of mill-dyed wools.

more. Most major fabric stores, rug-hooking stores and quilt shops carry mill-dyed woolens.

Selection of hand-dyed wools.

Hand-Dyed Wool

Hand-dyed wools are a wonderful choice for rug hooking because of the increasing variety of colors and the difference in mottling of colors on the wools. In rug hooking, mottled fabrics add dimension and color depth to your rugs.

Numerous companies hand-dye wool, all of which are unique and have their own styles. One thing to remember when purchasing hand-dyed wools is to purchase all you think you might need at once. The hand-dyeing process is ever-changing with one dye pot different from the next. Just as wallpaper or fabrics have dye lots, one batch of hand-dyed wool may vary in color from the next.

Choose your hand-dyed wools carefully. Be sure the wool is not stiff. Buy from experienced dyers because they take care to not over-heat the wools, which will cause the wool to "felt up," making it hard and unusable for rug hooking. Request color samples when possible, not only so you can see the colors available from the different vendors, but so you also can feel the wools. You'll learn over time that your sense of touch is important in rug hooking. Just feeling the fabric will aid you in knowing if the wool is a usable fabric for rug hooking.

Recycled Wool

Never turn down anybody's offer to give you wool garments or stash. Take anything you can get your hands on. If it doesn't work for you, either donate it to charity or pass it on to the next rug hooker. I've learned from past experience to accept everything graciously.

During your resale shop and rummage sale ventures, stay away from garments that are just too worn out or are extremely soiled and stained. Read the clothing labels and weed out garments with too high of a synthetic percentage. Check all wool jackets carefully to be sure the interfacing that is used on the inside of the garment is not permanently attached; clothing manufacturers adhere this interfacing directly to the wool, making it impossible to remove or to hook with.

Before storing your garment purchases, wash the items. Do not bring unwashed items near your other wool "stashes." Moths have a way of hiding in clothing fibers and you don't need these little critters anywhere near your other good woolens.

Once clean, take the garments apart, remove all zippers and buttons, and save only the usable wool pieces.

How Much?

How much wool will you need? In rug hooking, you need to estimate the amount of fabric needed to hook and this depends on how high you pull your loops up. Normally, you will use about four to five times the wool for the area you are hooking (more if you pull your loops very high). For example, if you are hooking a 2" square, you will need approximately 16 to 20 square inches of wool. Always estimate the amount of wool you need on the high side.

Recycled woolens.

Care and Storage of Wool

Normal commercial detergents keep the dreaded moth bug away and many wool fabrics, such as Dorr wool, are already "moth proof." When wool is properly washed with a mild detergent, such as Tide, in warm water, whether by hand or machine, followed by a cool water rinse and thorough drying, you can feel safe against moth damage.

Hand-dyed woolens have already been properly taken care of by most wool vendors you purchase from and do not need to be washed and dried once they are part of your collection.

Mill-dyed wool and recycled garments must be washed and dried before using. Not only to moth-proof them, but also to felt the fabrics.

Felting wool is not difficult. Simply wash in warm water, rinse in cold water and dry, and you will have felted your wool for rug hooking.

Be careful when drying, as too much heat will create a stiff wool that is unusable in rug hooking. High heat in the dryer is not necessary. Simply toss your wet woolens into the dryer with an old towel, which helps prevent wrinkles and gives just enough friction for the wool fibers to tighten up. All dryer settings are different, but try a medium heat and check on the piece every 20 minutes or so.

The same holds true for your water temperature in the washer. There is no need to use hot water, as a warm water setting works well.

Tara's Tip: On occasion, you will run across a loosely woven wool that needs more felting after the initial washing and drying. Simply rewash the fabric, using warm water again, but this time set the washer on a longer wash cycle so the wool can be agitated more.

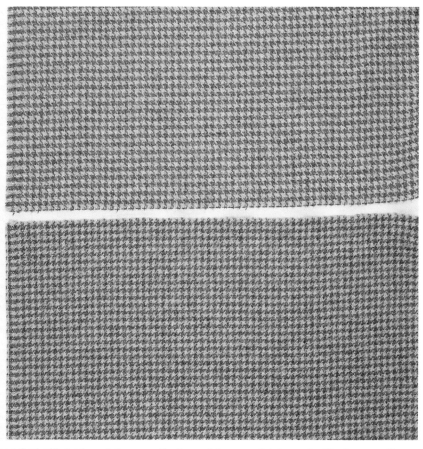

Unwashed mill-dyed wool shown on the top and the same fabric washed is shown on the bottom. Notice how the fibers in this wool have shrunk or "felted," making the overall pattern of the wool appear smaller.

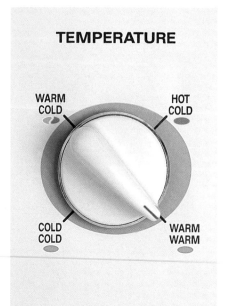

TEMPERATURE

Adjust the washer setting to warm so that the wool does not get too stiff during the washing process.

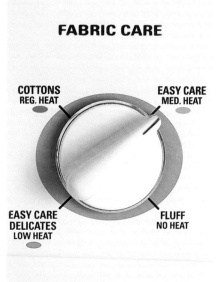

FABRIC CARE

Adjust the dryer setting to medium heat when drying wool.

Fabric softeners can be used to prevent static cling and to help soften the texture of certain wools.

Fabric softeners, whether added to your washer or as a dryer sheet into the dryer are optional. Use fabric softeners to help prevent static cling and to soften any rougher feeling wools.

Clean out the lint trap on your dryer after each load. Lint can build up from wool fabric in a short amount of time and create a fire hazard in your machine.

Some rug hookers prefer to store their wools in plastic containers or clear bags, while others use cupboards or shelves for storage. If care has already been taken to ward off moths, the storage of your wools is a personal choice.

You may want to categorize your wools by color or textures. Pick a system that works for you and the storage space that you have.

Take care to store your wools away from direct sunlight to help in the prevention of fabric fading. If you choose to store your wool in plastic containers or bags, keep them in a cool, dry place. Any moisture that might accumulate inside these bags or containers can cause your wool to mildew.

Always save any small remnants of wool or extra strips for future projects. Try storing these bits and pieces in small baskets or glass jars and use them for decoration.

Be sure to clean out your dryer's lint trap often to prevent fires.

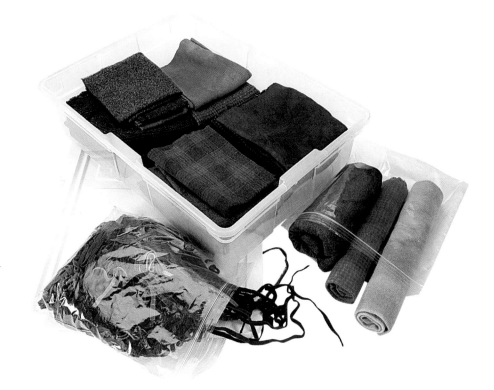

Storing wool, whether in containers, bags or on shelves, is simple and a personal choice.

Alternate Fabrics for Rug Hooking

Other fabrics and fibers can be introduced to your rug hooking projects.

Homespun Fabrics

Variety in colors and styles of plaids make 100 percent cotton homespun fabrics an attractive alternative to wool. This type of fabric is best for outlining in your rug hooking projects or for adding spark to your rugs.

Try cutting ½" to ¾" strips of homespun and fold them in half lengthwise to hook with. By folding the fabric in half and hooking it, you will give the homespun more bulk and make filling in the hooking area go more quickly. This is also an excellent trick to remember when hooking with thin wools.

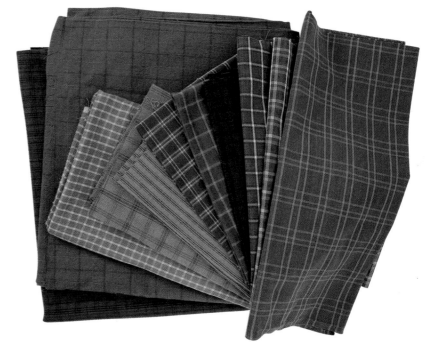

Homespun fabrics.

Vintage Laces and Trims

Try hooking a bit of lace into your rugs and watch the visual sensations come alive. Just the texture and dimensions that are added by using laces and trims in small areas makes a rug very pleasing to the eye.

Nylons and Silk Stockings

Nylons and silk stockings have been used for years in rug hooking and both can even be dyed, using the correct type of dyes. Though the fabrics are thin, you can cut wider strips and fold them to hook with. New rug hookers should experiment with nylons and silk stockings after getting the basics down, as these materials stretch and can be a bit trying at first.

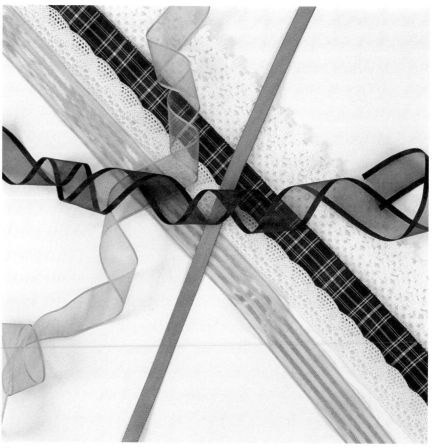

Vintage laces and trims.

Wool Yarns

There are so many different colors and thicknesses of wool yarn that it's unbelievable. Yarn is not only an appealing addition to a rug, but it is also easy to find. Try a nice thick rugger's yarn or a variety of nubby yarns. Again, new hookers should get the basics down first before attempting to hook with yarn.

Sheep Hair/ Wool Fibers

Actual raw sheep hair or wool fibers can also be hooked into your rugs. Visit the doll-making section of your local craft store and purchase a package of 100 percent wool mohair. The fibers can be a bit tricky to hook with, but add a nice twist to your rug. Use a great, strong red to hook a doll's or child's hair section or a great natural gray or brown shade to hook part of a sheep's coat.

Nylons and silk stockings.

100 percent wool yarns.

Raw sheep's wool and fibers.

Chapter 3

Color Choices

The color wheel plays an important part in rug hooking if you choose to dye some of your own wool fabrics. With the use of this inexpensive tool and some simple thinking, your rugs will look fabulous every time.

Color Theory

Throughout the next few pages you will read and learn many things about color in general. The information included in this chapter will be applied while you are color planning your rugs and also when dyeing your wool fabrics.

Color theory is the study of how colors relate to one another, which is also known as "color harmony." Harmony is a pleasing arrangement of colors. It engrosses the viewer and creates a sense of order or a balance in what is being looked at. When something isn't harmonious, it's either a bore to look at or very disorderly or chaotic. Visually you need to create harmony and balance in your rugs so that they are easy to look at and derive some sense of order. Whether you enjoy creating the primitive style of rugs depicted in this book or if you are a fine art hooker, you need color balance in your projects.

Why do some colors look great together while others just hurt your eyes? Why is one color so pretty and lovely alone and looks washed out or faded when used with another color? These are the types of dilemmas you might face during rug hooking and dyeing. Knowing how colors relate to each other and choosing the right ones can make or break your project.

The Basic Color Wheel

The color wheel brings back memories from grade school, but as simple as it looks, it's still a very important tool while hooking and dyeing. A simple color wheel helps in understanding similarities and differences in color. Color wheels show how the colors are related to each other. Primary, secondary and intermediate colors are organized on a circular chart. By using a color wheel, you can visibly see how to mix and think about colors.

Invest in a simple, inexpensive color wheel, like the one shown here. You can find simple color wheels at your local arts and crafts store. A basic wheel is great to start out with, but over time, you will want to upgrade to a more detailed wheel.

The primary colors are red, blue and yellow. Primary colors cannot be made from other colors and are considered pure colors. Secondary and intermediate colors are created by mixing primary colors.

The secondary colors are green, orange and violet (purple). Two primary colors mix to form a secondary color. Each secondary color is made from the two primary colors on either side of it in the color wheel, as shown in the diagram. Red and yellow will produce orange; yellow and blue will make green; and red and blue will give you purple.

The intermediate colors, sometimes known as the tertiary colors, are made by mixing a secondary and a primary color together, as shown on the accompanying diagram. Blue-green, yellow-orange, red-orange, yellow-green, blue-violet and red-violet are all examples of intermediate colors.

Here are a few other terms to remember when rug hooking and dyeing:

Analogous colors: Colors that are next to each other on the color wheel. They are closely related because they have a certain color in common. For example, blue, blue-green and green all contain blue. Red, orange and yellow are analogous colors because red and yellow make orange.

Complementary colors: Colors that are opposite of each other on the color wheel. When you use complementary colors next to each

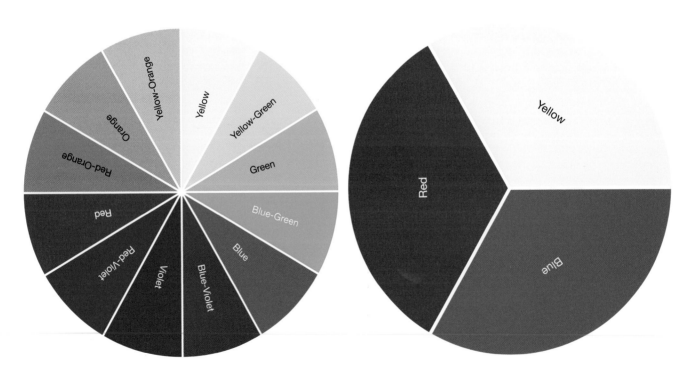

A Standard Color Wheel

The primary colors are red, blue and yellow.

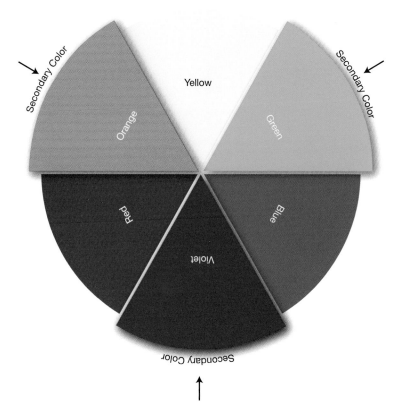

other or side-by-side in a hooked rug, the colors intensify each other. For example, orange and blue are opposite of each other on the color wheel, as shown, and when hooked together, they work well and intensify each other.

Tara's Tip: *It is not necessary only to use the exact opposite to create the same effect of harmony in your rugs. For a yellow flower, if you were to hook the center purple, you wouldn't have to use the exact opposite value of violet. You can use one of purple's analogous colors, such as a blue-violet to add a more cool tone to your flower or a red-violet to add a warmer feel. This is important to remember when using complementary colors in your rugs. You don't want to create a tug of war effect between colors, and by using the complementary colors equally in a rug, they manage to compete for attention. Let one of the colors dominate the other to create a more pleasing effect.*

The intermediate colors are blue-green, yellow-orange, red-orange, yellow-green, blue-violet and red-violet.

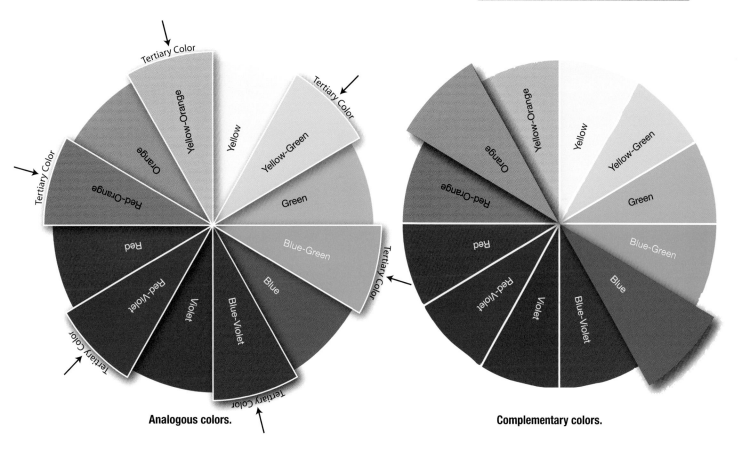

Analogous colors.

Complementary colors.

Cool/warm colors: All colors can be warm, cool or neutral. Cool colors have more blue and less red or yellow (think nighttime, winter or a cool lake). Warm colors have more red or yellow and less blue (think daytime, summer, fire or brilliant fall leaves).

For example, using your color wheel and mixing green with a higher amount of yellow, you create a warm yellow-green shade, as shown.

Mix green with a higher amount of blue and you create a cool blue-green shade, as shown.

Red is pure and neutral. Add yellow to red and you make orange, a very warm color, as shown.

Mix blue with red and create violet, as shown, which is very cool.

Black, white, gray, off-whites and light beiges are considered neutral and work well in all color harmonies.

Hue: The name of a color. When you blend the hues blue and yellow, as shown, you create another hue—green.

Intensity: The brightness, or purity, of a color and the dullness, or saturation, of a color. For example,

yellow is brighter, or more pure, than gold. Navy blue is more dull or saturated than blue. Lower the intensity of a color by adding white or black.

Shade: A dark value. Add black to a color to create a shade. For example, burgundy forms when black is added to red, as shown.

Tint: A light value. Add white to a color to create light values. For example, lilac forms when white is added to violet or purple, as shown.

Value: The amount of light or dark in a color/hue. Baby pink is a light value of red, as shown, while burgundy is a dark value of red.

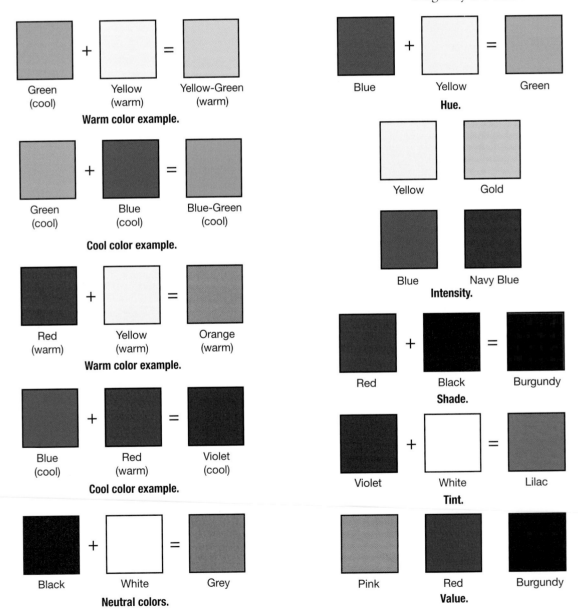

Green (cool) + Yellow (warm) = Yellow-Green (warm)
Warm color example.

Green (cool) + Blue (cool) = Blue-Green (cool)
Cool color example.

Red (warm) + Yellow (warm) = Orange (warm)
Warm color example.

Blue (cool) + Red (warm) = Violet (cool)
Cool color example.

Black + White = Grey
Neutral colors.

Blue + Yellow = Green
Hue.

Yellow   Gold

Blue   Navy Blue
Intensity.

Red + Black = Burgundy
Shade.

Violet + White = Lilac
Tint.

Pink   Red   Burgundy
Value.

Using Color Theory

How does all this color theory relate to your rug-hooking project? Many beginning rug hookers wonder about what color to use and where they should be placed within the project.

The key is to follow your heart and not become frustrated. After you have chosen your pattern and decide basically what color scheme you want to use, start playing! Have fun and pull colors from your wool stash that you like and would love to see used in your new hooking project. Spread your chosen fabrics out and view them from a distance and close-up. What works well together and what does not? Be sure to view the colors standing back at a distance, as your eyes will see things differently and most of the time, this is how your finished rug will be viewed.

Place your chosen colors around on your rug pattern approximately where they will go when hooked. (This works well on larger rugs and is a little more difficult on small rugs or mats.) What you want to create is a balance of color in your rug. For example, in the American Symbol rug project, there is a "triangle" of color that promotes balance. A triangle of color means that one color is hooked in a triangular view on your rug, as shown in the accompanying photo. Notice the eagle beak is hooked in gold as are the centers of each pomegranate. The balance goes further, as the eagle's feet are hooked in gold, which creates another visual triangle of color between the eagle's beak, the feet and the pomegranates.

Triangles of color do not need to be used a million times throughout

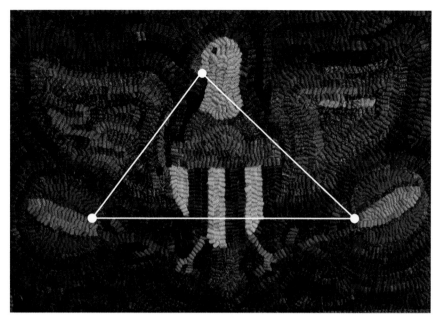

"Triangle of color" in the American Symbol rug shows how balance is created.

your rugs, once or twice for a nice balance is fine. The colors are placed throughout the rugs to create a nice flow that is pleasing to your eye and helps to prevent too many colors or objects in a rug from competing for attention.

With that said, you will often create rugs where it is impossible to use triangles of color and that is fine. Smaller mats and hooked items generally have a life of their own and their main focus typically is one object in the rug. For example, in My Flurry Friend, shown here and detailed on page 108, it would have been more of a challenge to place a triangle of color in this mat. The snowman itself makes enough statement and is not competing with so many other colors. The color balance in this small rug works fine.

When choosing your rug colors, remember to pay attention to the warmness or coolness of the colors selected. What would you prefer to see in the rug—more warm shades or cool? Do you have a complementary color picked out

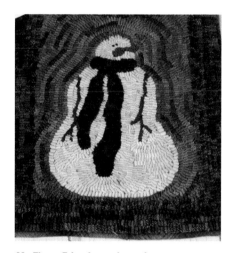

My Flurry Friend rug shows how a rug can work even without the existence of a triangle of color.

to add some intensity to certain areas of your rug? Choose colors that flow well together, as drastic color changes can look jumpy and chaotic.

In a cool color scheme (greens, violets and blues), the cool colors must dominate your project. To break this down even further— to have good color harmony— one dominant cool color must dominate over the others. For example, in a hooked rug that depicts an ocean sunset theme,

Sometimes, the original plan for background colors changes as the design evolves, as it did with the American Symbol rug.

Notice how the border colors of the Love Never Melts rug blend nicely with the main motif and do not take away from it.

At times the center motif in a rug is powerful, yet understated enough that the overall rug can handle having several new colors added in the border.

the dominant cool color could be a gorgeous shade of blue-green for the water, with highlights of cool violet shades and cool green shades throughout the ocean and farther off into the distance.

Move on in your ocean theme and add a complementary color. With blue-green as the dominant cool color, orange would be the hue to harmonize this rug. Orange is also a warm color, so use it wisely and not as prominently. Let's say in your sunset over this ocean there are casts of orange where the sun is setting. Use minor amounts of orange to complement the blue-green ocean, yet not distract from it.

What about the background color? Some people pick background colors first, while others wait until the end. This is a personal choice. For example for the American Symbol rug, shown here and detailed on page 66, the original plan was to hook the background in natural, light tan and oatmeal shades. After hooking the pomegranates and then the eagle, however, it became apparent the eagle and pomegranates would have become washed out with the original background shades. The black shade works much better.

Never take your background colors for granted. If a background is too light or too dark, it can ultimately wash out or take over your rug completely.

Always try to carry some of the colors from your rug into your outside borders. It's not wise to introduce a new color in the border area, because the new color normally will compete with the actual design itself. This is true for rugs that have one main center focus with very few colors used. In the Love Never Melts rug, shown here and detailed on page 113, few colors were used to hook the center motif, so if a new color were introduced in the border, it would have

competed with the design itself.

Sometimes it is possible to bring in a few new colors in the border. For example, in the Folk Art Horse rug, several new colors were added to the border, yet the overall rug remains pleasing. When the center design is powerful and neutral and non competing colors are used, the rug can handle the addition of new colors in the border. As long as the colors in the border work well with the overall coolness or warmness of your rug, everything will run smoothly. Introducing bright primary or pastel colors to the border would not have worked well in this example. Such colors would have created friction and competition in the rug.

Suggestions for Using Color

The focus of the projects in this book is on more primitive-style hooked rugs. As such, most of the colors selected tend to be more true-to-life than whimsical. That means cats use browns, blacks, reds, whites or grays. Water is always blue and cows are always black, white, and brown or reddish-colored.

Remember that things do not always have to be hooked as they actually are. It all depends on your style and taste. Crows can be purple, cats can be bright red, chickens can be blue, pumpkins can be a cast of green and so on.

In primitive rug hooking, a childlike quality tends to shine through. If whimsical is more your style, think as a child would. What do you see through a child's eye?

The following are a few suggestions for using color in your rugs:

Trees: Greens, browns, tans and some great earth-tone plaids.

Flowers: The possibilities are endless. Flowers are virtually every color under the sun. They are a good place to practice using complementary colors. Hook gold flowers with a great red-violet outline. Hook burnt orange flowers with a stunning cool blue plaid fabric. Hook lovely primitive red flowers outlined in olive green wools.

Leaves: Reds, oranges, greens and yellows.

Pumpkins: Oranges, tans, whites, greens and yellows.

Snow and snowmen: Oatmeals, light tans, dirty-looking white, light grays, and tea-stained colors.

Oceans: Blues, violets and blue-greens.

Chickens: Black-and-white checks; rust reds; great plaids that are blue, green or teal; and red, white and gray checks.

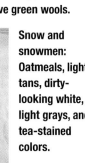

Skies: Blues, violets, blue-greens and red-violets.

Hills and grass: Yellows, greens, browns, green plaids, brown plaids, tans and reddish browns.

Flags: Blue-and-white houndstooths are great to give the impression of twinkling stars in the blue area of flags. Several different shades of red make the flag appear to be waving. Creams and oatmeals for the white stripes.

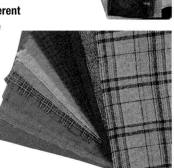

Houses: Great small red plaids; gray tweeds; tan-and-white houndstooths; blues; and light browns.

Birds: Reds, blues, golds, greens, whites, blacks, grays and violets.

Dyeing

Dyeing your own wool fabrics will allow you to have more control over your projects. Your creativity will start to bloom—along with your stash of wool!

Dyeing wool is not a necessity when rug hooking, but it does have its benefits. By learning to dye your own wools, you will learn more about the entire color process and how certain colors react when mixed together. Dyeing also gives you the ability to have the right colors on hand when you need them. Further, it allows you to change virtually any color of wool into something more usable.

Dyeing is fun. Once you learn the basics, you'll be off on a dyeing tangent because of the excitement you'll feel from creating your own hand-dyed wool.

Don't worry. Dyeing is not for everyone and if you choose not to dye your own wool, there are still other ways to hook without creating the hand-dyed wools yourself. Many rug hooking and quilting stores, online shops and individuals offer hand-dyed wools.

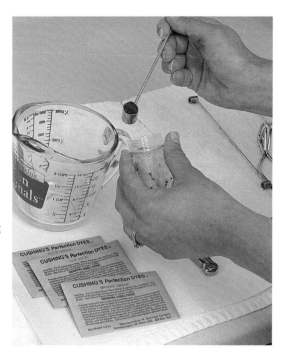

Supplies Needed

The main thing to remember when gathering or purchasing your dye supplies is that they will be used just for dyeing purposes. Never reuse any item for preparing food once you have used it in dyeing. With this in mind, make a special place to store your dye equipment so that no one in your household will confuse these items and use them in food preparation.

The following is a basic list of the supplies you will need. Some supplies will be used more than others, and some may not be used at all, depending on the type of dyeing you choose to do.

Read this entire section on dyeing before attempting it so that you are more familiar with all the steps involved before approaching them.

Bleach or Bleach Wipes

Spills will occur and dyes will float in the air, so be sure to have bleach or bleach wipes on hand to clean up after your dyeing session is over.

Remember to keep these chemicals away from your dye pots. Refrain from cleaning the dye area until you are finished dyeing for the day. Even the smallest contact of these chemicals to the wool can create a nasty white spot on the wools.

Dust Mask

Always try to wear a dust mask when dyeing. The tiny particles of dye are very fine and can easily be inhaled.

Dyes

There are several different brands of chemical dyes on the market today. In this book, W. Cushing Acid Dyes are recommended (see Resources, page 128).

Dye Pots

You will need two 10- to 12-quart enamel or stainless steel pots for dyeing your wools. White enamel pots work the best so that you can see the dyes and the wools in the pot while preparing them.

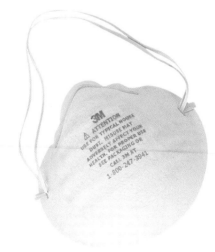

Glass Measuring Cup

Purchase a sturdy glass 2-cup measuring cup. It will be needed to mix the dyes prior to adding them to the dye pots.

Measuring Spoons

Use special dye spoons to measure out the dyes. There are several companies that produce these spoons.

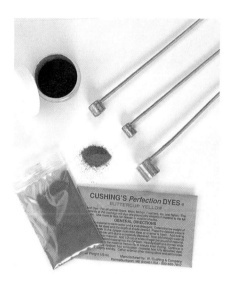

Notebook/Paper Pad/Note Cards and Pen

Keep a notebook, pad of paper or note cards and a pen near you while dyeing so you can keep track of any new recipes you create. Write down notes or keep track of your dyeing results for future use.

Old Clothes or Apron

Be sure to wear old clothing, or at least cover your clothing up with a large, long apron. Splashes can occur while dyeing and the dye can be rather difficult to remove once it sets into your clothes.

Old Towels and Rags

You'll need a good supply of old towels or rags on hand to wipe up any spills. Having one or two towels lying on your countertops is a good idea, as they make good places to rest your dye spoons and measure out dyes. By spritzing the towel with a little water, it will actually catch and hold some of the floating dye particles that are in the air.

Potholders

Use good, thick potholders to lift your pots after the wools are finished.

Rubber Gloves

There are two different kinds of gloves that are good for dyeing wool. The best would be a pair of Bluettes, which can easily be found at your local hardware store. Bluettes gloves are insulated, thus protecting your hands from the extreme heat of the water used to dye wool. Buy them a size larger than you normally would so that they slip on and off your hands easily while dyeing.

Normal thin surgical type gloves can also be used to protect your fingers from the dye particles when measuring out dyes. The dye particles will not harm you. They will just turn your fingers temporarily a different color.

Spoons

Metal or wooden spoons are great for stirring your dye solutions once they are in the dye pot. The old white enamel spoons are the best so that you can see the actual colors in the cup of the spoon, but they are difficult to find today. Stainless steel spoons or simple wooden spoons are the next best options.

Table Salt

Normal common table salt is used to clean the dye particles off of your dye spoons quickly. Place a small amount into a clean baby food jar or small container and swish your dye spoon through the salt to clean.

Tongs

Metal tongs are a great tool to have on hand for lifting and turning the wool while it is in the dye pot.

Vinegar or Citric Acid Crystals

Normal white vinegar from your local grocery store is needed to "set" the colors permanently into the wool fabrics. Such a setting solution is also commonly called the "mordant" when dyeing wool.

Another mordant that can be used when dyeing wool is citric acid crystals. Crystals are a little more expensive and not as easy to buy quickly, but they can be purchased through many rug hooking shops and online chemical and dye companies. Citric acid crystals have no odor, as vinegar does, which is the biggest benefit to using them.

Wetting Agents

Wool fabrics need to soak in water that has a small amount of a wetting agent added to it before dyeing. A wetting agent will help the cuticles of the wool fully open so that the dyes can better penetrate the wool fiber.

There are several different wetting agents to choose from. A common commercial wetting agent is Wetter Than Wet. By using this wetting agent, the wool will be ready to dye within about five minutes of soaking time. Jet Dry is another, more common product you can use that will have the wool ready to dye in about 5 minutes.

Ivory dish soap can easily be found at your local grocery store, as well as normal Tide liquid detergent. When using either Ivory dish soap or normal, nothing-added Tide liquid detergent as wetting agents, be sure to let the wools soak for a minimum of 45 minutes.

If your wool happens to soak longer than suggested, no harm will be done to your wools.

Preparing the Wool

Any wool that you will be dyeing, even one that has been previously washed, needs to be properly soaked in a solution of water and wetting agent. Wool is naturally resistant to water and that is why you need to use a wetting agent. Presoaking wool in water with a wetting agent added will open the wool cuticles up and allows the dyes to completely enter the wool fibers. If the wool is not properly presoaked, you could end up with what is commonly called "white core" wool. White core is a white or undyed area of the wool between the top and bottom surfaces.

1. Begin by tearing your wool into the desired-size pieces needed in your dye recipes. The dye recipes in this book require one fat quarter of wool per recipe. A fat quarter of wool is easily achieved by snipping and tearing the wool fabric on grain, as follows:

- With 1 yard of wool in front of you, measure the selvedge edge of the wool to be sure you have a full 36" length of wool. Wools commonly measure 58" in width.
- Fold your yard-long piece of wool and find the center or ½-yard mark of the 36" side of the wool.
- Snip the wool at this ½-yard mark and tear the piece in half.
- Fold one of your ½-yard pieces in half again, this time matching the selvedge edges. The selvedge edges are the edges that now measure 18" wide.
- Along the fold, make a snip in the wool and tear the wool in half. You should end up with a fat quarter of wool that measures approximately 18" wide x 29" long.

2. Add a wetting agent into a bath of water in your kitchen sink and soak the piece of wool for the time necessary, depending on the agent used. See Wetting Agents, page 36, for guidance.

3. When the wool is finished soaking, empty the water from the kitchen sink or washer and squeeze out all excess water. The wool is now ready to dye.

Preparing the Dye Area

Setting up a dye area is simple. The basic rule is to have everything you need within arm's reach. Place towels down on your countertops and then arrange your dye supplies so that you can see everything and find it easily. Keep your individual dye packets or containers away from the sink or water areas so they don't get wet accidentally.

Dyeing in Larger Quantities

When I know I will be dyeing, I'll soak a large amount of wool (generally 8 to 10 yards) in my washing machine, rather than the sink, with about a ½-cup of Tide laundry detergent overnight. If you choose to dye in bulk, here's how:

1. Set your washing machine for a full load capacity and start filling the drum with water.
2. Add ½-cup of Tide.
3. Once the washer is filled, allow it to agitate for a minute or two to really mix the detergent around.
4. Add your wool, making sure it is pushed all the way down into the water.
5. Turn the washing machine back on and allow it to agitate for a minute or so.
6. Turn the machine off and allow the wools to soak.

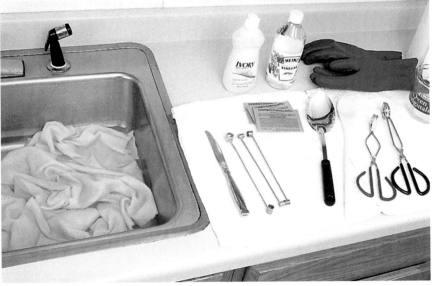

Example of a dye area setup.

Dyeing the Wool

Dye particles can settle in their containers before being used.

1. Mix the dry dyes in the small plastic envelopes before measuring them.

2. Bring approximately 1½ cups of water to a boil in a small pan and keep a steady slow boil going until the water is needed.

3. Measure the dry dyes needed for your chosen recipe into the 2-cup glass measuring cup using the necessary dye spoon.

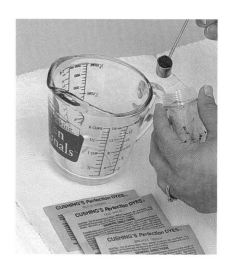

Measure dry dyes.

4. Level the top of the dye spoon off with the flat side of a butter knife, as shown, to get a more accurate measurement.

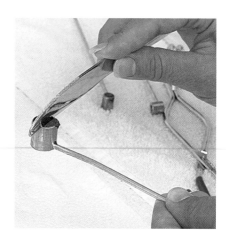

Level off the dye.

5. Add necessary dyes to the measuring cup, followed by a few drops of water and stir to create a paste. Use the edge of the butter knife so that you can be sure to break up all clumps of dyes and scrape the sides of the glass measuring cup.

Make a paste from the dyes and a small amount of water.

6. Add the boiling water and stir the solution until all dye particles have dissolved completely.

Add water to make the dye paste into a dye solution.

7. Add warm water to a 10- to 12-quart dye pot, filling the pot one-third full of water. By filling the pot with this much water, the wool will have less room to move around,

which will help create a great mottle appearance. If you prefer more of a solid-colored wool, add more water to your dye pot and stir constantly.

8. Add dye solution to water in the dye pot and set the pot on the stove burner.

Add dye solution to pots.

9. Turn the stove on medium heat, stir the solution to be sure the dyes are mixed well throughout the pot.

10. Scrunch the fat quarter of wool up slightly and add it to the dye pot.

Add wool to dye pot.

11. Use tongs or a long handled spoon to push the wool down below the water level so that the dyes can penetrate the wool. Some of the wool will float back above the water after being mashed down and that is OK.

Push wool below the water's surface.

12. Allow wool to soak for approximately five minutes and then use the tongs to lift the wool and turn it so that the side of the wool that was closest to the burner is now on the top nearest the top of the water level.

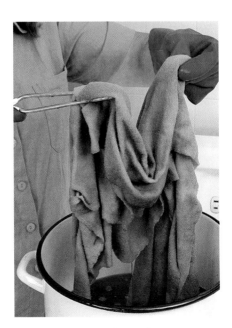

Check and turn wool in the dye pot.

13. Check the dye solution in the dye pot. If most of the dye solution has soaked into the wool, add ⅛-cup vinegar or mordant to the pot and stir to mix.

Add vinegar to dye pot.

14. Allow wool to stew for 20 to 30 minutes, until the dye bath is almost or completely clear again.

15. Turn the burner off on the stove.

16. Use your tongs to remove the wool from the dye bath, place it in the sink to cool and rinse the newly dyed wool with warm water, slowly changing the water to cold. You don't want to "shock" the wool with cold water automatically because this can cause the wool fibers to shrink too much, resulting in hard or over-felted wool. Meanwhile, let the remaining dye pot water cool before dumping it in the sink.

Cool dyed wool in the sink.

17. Squeeze the excess water from the dyed wool. You have the option of running the wool through the spin cycle of your washing machine to help get as much of the water out of the wool before drying.

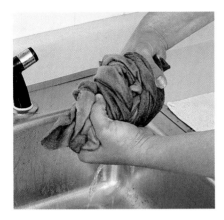

Squeeze excess water from dyed wool.

18. Air-dry or dry wool in the dryer on a medium setting. If using the dryer, toss in an old towel to help prevent wrinkles. Adding a dryer sheet will not hurt either and can help make the wool softer and fresh-smelling. Check the dryer every 15 minutes or so to see if the wool is dry and also to clean out the dryer vent. Wool fibers will collect quickly in the vent as the wool is drying.

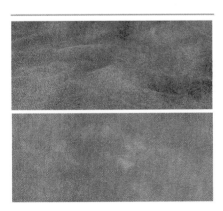

Same piece of dyed wool when wet (top) and dried.

Tara's Tip: *Remember when checking your wool during the dyeing process that wet wool will appear darker in color than when it is dry.*

Using Prepared Color Recipes

Several different dye recipes follow for you to use in your rug-hooking projects. These dye recipes were used to dye several of the wools you see in the projects in this book. Each of the dye recipes is used to dye one fat quarter of wool. Experiment with each and use different shades of wool to create many different shades of each color. In the accompanying photos, the recipes are shown dyed over natural-colored wool unless otherwise noted.

Khaki Meadow

¼ tsp. Khaki Drab
1⁄16 tsp. Tan
1⁄64 tsp. Bronze Green

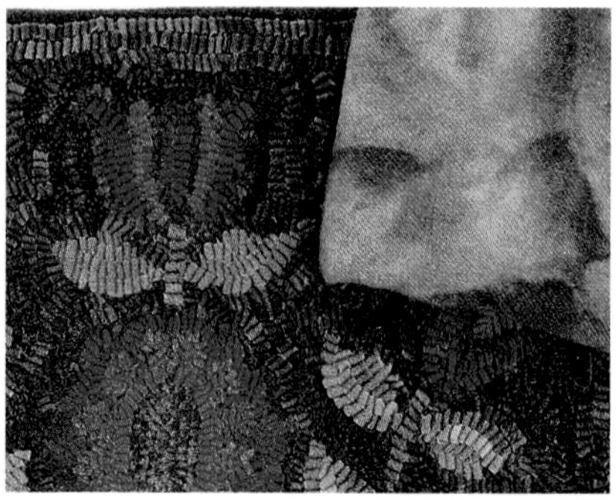

Khaki Meadow.

Blue Madness

⅛ plus 1⁄16 tsp. Blue
⅛ tsp. Peacock
1⁄64 tsp. Dark Gray

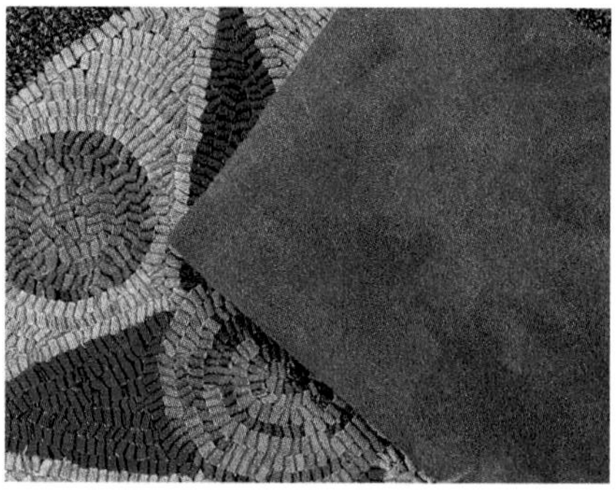

Blue Madness (shown dyed over light gray wool).

Butter Cream

¼ tsp. Old Ivory
⅛ tsp. Maize
1⁄128 tsp. Medium Brown
1⁄128 tsp. Old Gold

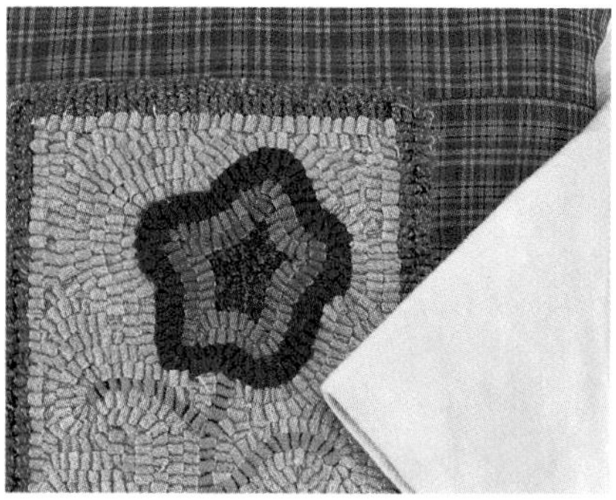

Butter Cream.

Primitive Black

½ tsp. Olive Green
¼ tsp. Spice Brown
⅛ tsp. Black
⅛ tsp. Silver Gray Green

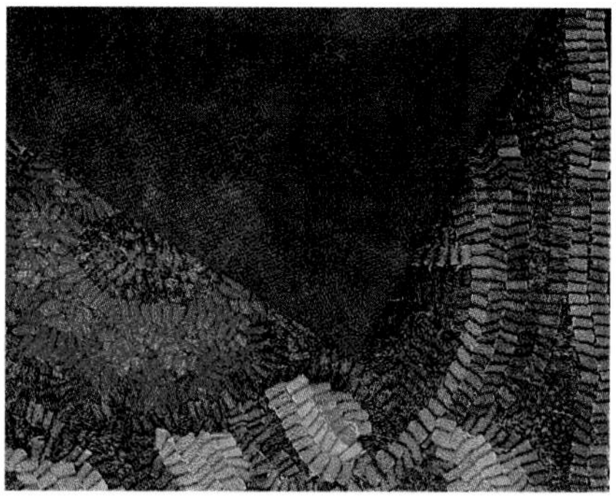

Primitive Black.

Primitive Red

¼ tsp. Terra Cotta
¼ tsp. Mulberry
¼ tsp. Khaki Drab

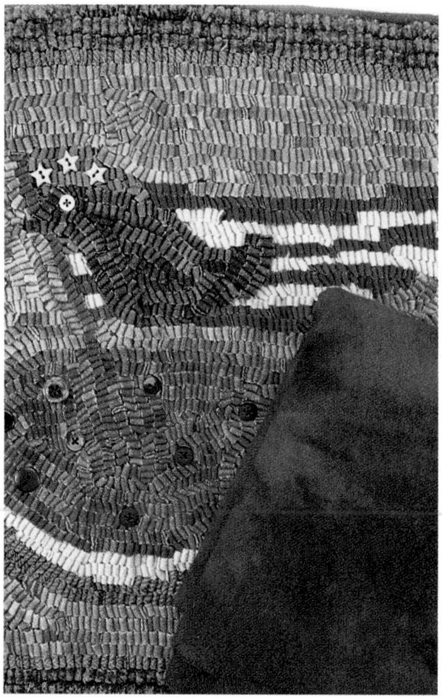

Primitive Red.

Tree Bark

¼ plus ⅛ tsp. Canary
¼ tsp. Dark Brown
1⁄32 plus 1⁄64 tsp. Khaki Drab
1⁄32 plus 1⁄64 tsp. Mummy Brown

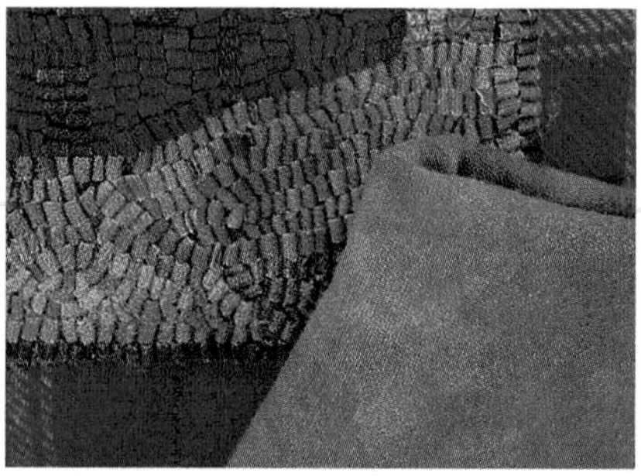

Tree Bark.

Eggplant

⅛ plus 1⁄16 tsp. Reseda Green
⅛ plus 1⁄16 tsp. Crimson
1⁄16 plus 1⁄32 Plum

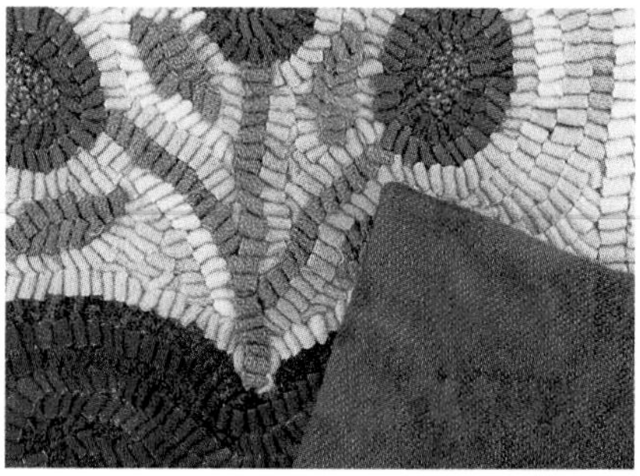

Eggplant.

Marrying and Stewing Wools

Marrying and stewing are two types of dyeing that can be done without the use of any commercial dyes. Both of these dyeing methods can involve using mill-dyed wools, recycled woolens and even hand-dyed wools that just turn out to be the wrong shade.

Stewing to Remove Color

Stewing wool to remove color involves using a piece of wool that might be too bright or simply just not the right shade. For example, a bright fuchsia-colored wool can be stewed to remove some of the excess dye, bringing the color of wool to something that may be a bit more to your taste. Stewing can lighten colors, but will not remove the color completely.

1. Fill a 10- to 12-quart dye pot half full with water and place it on the stove.

2. Fill a second 10- to 12-quart dye pot half full with water and add ¼-cup of white vinegar per quarter yard of wool. Place the second dye pot on the stove and bring it to a simmer.

3. Add 1 Tbsp. of normal Tide laundry detergent per fat quarter that will be stewed to the first dye pot (the one without vinegar in it). Stir the pot so that the detergent and the water are completely blended.

4. Add the wool that needs to be lightened. There is no reason to presoak the wool that will be stewed. Be sure there is plenty of room in the pot for the wool to move around easily.

5. Bring the pot of wool to a simmer, but do not let it boil. Stir the pot every five to 10 minutes or so. Stirring will help to circulate the wool in the water and the Tide mixture, which will aid in the dye release from the fabric.

6. Check the wool every several minutes by wearing Bluette gloves and lifting the wool out of the pot with tongs. Squeeze some of the excess water from the wool to see if it is a shade that is more suitable to you.

7. Remove the wool from the pot once it is the desired color and place it in the second dye pot (the one with vinegar).

8. Simmer the wool in the vinegar water for 20 to 30 minutes, stirring periodically.

9. Remove the wool from the pot and place it in the sink to cool.

10. Rinse the wool in warm water, gradually changing the water temperature to cool.

11. Squeeze out excess water or run through the spin cycle in your washing machine.

12. Air-dry or use the dryer on a medium heat setting with a towel to prevent wrinkling. Check your wool and clean the dryer vent every 15 minutes or so.

Marrying Colors

Stewing to marry wool is an easy concept. Stew several different colors of wool together so that they work better together in a project. You can use several different shades in the same color family or use colors of wool that are total opposites or in different color families.

Two pieces of wool shown before marrying colors (left) and after. Notice how the color of the stewed piece on the right is more vibrant.

For example, you can stew some reds, pinks, tans, bright pinks and burgundys to create varying degrees of pink to burgundy.

Stew some bright orange with a small piece of blue (this is where your color wheel knowledge will come in handy). By stewing these two colors, the orange will become more subdued because you are using complementary colors together in the dye pot.

When choosing wools to marry together, pay attention to the dark or deep colors you are adding to the pot. These dark wools have considerably more dye in them than light-colored wool. Often, such darker wools can release a lot of dye and overtake the color in the dye pot. Experimentation is the best teacher. Start with smaller pieces of the darker or more dominant shade, as you can always add more later.

1. Fill a 10- to 12-quart dye pot half full with water and place it on the stove.

2. Add 2 Tbsp. of normal Tide laundry detergent per fat quarter that will be stewed. (This is not an exact science; you can add more Tide if necessary or lessen the amount according to the amount of wool in the pot. Generally use about a tablespoon of detergent per fat quarter.) Stir the pot so that the detergent and the water are completely blended.

3. Repeat steps 4 through 6 from the previous Stewing instructions, page 41.

4. Add ½-cup or more of white vinegar to the pot to set the desired color in the wool.

5. Repeat steps 8 through 12 from the previous Stewing instructions, page 41.

Tea-Stained Wool

Tea staining wool is a great way to achieve a light warm yellow or camel shade of wool that is perfect for a background color when starting with white or natural-colored wool. Tea staining can also be used over previously dyed wools to subdue the color a bit.

1. Place six regular-sized teabags in a 10- to 12-quart dye pot filled one-quarter full with water.

2. Bring water to a soft boil for 10 minutes.

3. Remove teabags and discard.

4. Fill the pot with more warm water until halfway full.

5. Reduce the heat and allow the water to reach a simmer level.

6. Add ½-yard wool that has already presoaked in a wetting agent

and simmer for 15 to 20 minutes, checking the wool at five-minute intervals for the desired color. The longer the wool remains in the tea bath, the darker it will be.

7. Add ¼-cup white vinegar to set the color when it is the desired shade and simmer another 15 to 20 minutes.

8. Remove the wool from the pot and place it in the sink to cool.

9. Rinse the wool in warm water, gradually changing the water temperature to cool.

10. Squeeze out excess water or run through the spin cycle in your washing machine.

11. Air-dry or use the dryer on a medium heat setting with a towel to prevent wrinkling. Check your wool and clean the dryer vent every 15 minutes or so.

Onionskin Wool

Onionskin dyeing is another way to achieve a beautiful background. In these examples, yellow onionskins were used. Also experiment with purple onionskins, as they too create a beautiful shade.

1. Cut one leg off a pair of old pantyhose that have been washed and dried.

2. Stuff the pantyhose leg with 6 to 8 cups of dry onionskins and tie closed at the top.

3. Fill a 10- to 12-quart dye pot half full with water and add the onionskin-filled hose.

4. Bring water to a simmer and maintain simmer for 30 minutes, stirring the skins frequently.

5. Remove the pantyhose and discard.

6. Fill the dye pot with more water until it is two-thirds full.

A tea-stained wool was used in the background color of the Floral Display project, shown here and detailed on pages 100 and 101.

7. Allow the onionskin bath to come to a simmer and add wools that have already presoaked in a wetting agent.

8. Push the wool down so that all of the fabric is immersed in the onionskin bath. Some wools will naturally come back above the water levels.

9. Simmer for approximately 20 minutes, making sure the water does not start to boil and stirring occasionally.

10. Add ¼- to a ½-cup white vinegar when desired color is achieved and stir.

11. Simmer the wool for an additional 15 to 20 minutes to set the color.

12. Repeat steps 8 through 11 from the Tea-Staining instructions, page 42.

Tara's Tip: Experiment with onionskins to marry a variety of unrelated colors of wool. This type of dyeing will add a nice warm, aged golden patina to mill-dyed or hand-dyed wools that you want to blend together better in a rug-hooking project. To marry wools using onionskins, follow the basic onionskin dyeing method.

Tara's No-Fuss Dyeing Method

Once you have been dyeing for a while, you are bound to want a quicker method of dyeing. The following is the method I devised for just such a purpose. This is my own personal method for dyeing wool. It's a bit quicker and the mottles in my wools are great. All of the wools that I have personally dyed and used throughout the projects in this book were created using this method.

1. Start with an old enamelware baby bathtub or smaller round enamelware dish pan that you can find in antique stores and resale shops. They should be at least 8" deep (varying widths are fine).

2. Pour water into the bottom of the tub or pan until it is about 1" deep.

3. Measure all dry dyes directly into the pots.

4. Turn on the stove burners and stir the dye mixture well.

5. Allow the mixture to come to a boil and bring it to a rapid boil for two to three minutes, so that all dye particles have been dissolved.

6. Pour warm water into the tub/pan until it is two-thirds full of water and bring to a simmer for five minutes.

7. Stir the dye bath a few times and with the wool already wet, submerge it into the dye bath.

8. Push the wool down so that it is submerged in the dye bath and allow to simmer for about five minutes.

9. Pour ¼-cup vinegar or add 1 tablespoon citric acid crystals into the dye bath.

10. Use tongs to lift and turn the wool over immediately after adding the vinegar or citric acid so the opposite side is now facing down. Remember: The heat is coming from the burner and the wool that is facing downward can and will get darker spots on it from the heat source. Sometimes this is a good thing and sometimes it is not, depending on the color you are trying to achieve.

11. Allow the wool to simmer until the dye bath is clear.

12. Repeat steps 8 through 11 from the Tea-Staining instructions, page 42.

Onionskin-dyed wool was used in the background for the Flag Footstool project, shown here and detailed on pages 110-112.

Chapter 4

Basic Techniques

Once you have gathered all the necessary supplies and decided on a pattern to hook, you need to learn the basic techniques that will bring your project to life. Such techniques are detailed in this chapter.

Cutting Wool Into Strips

There are several different ways to cut your wool into the strips of fabric needed for rug hooking. Beginners should use the simplest, least expensive method of cutting by hand.

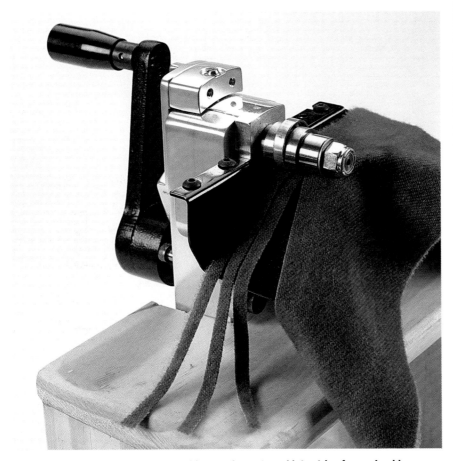

A mechanical cutter or "stripper" machine used to cut wool into strips for rug hooking.

Cutting by Hand

When cutting wool by hand, there are two different approaches.

Method 1

Use this method when you are going to hook in a #8 or ¼" strip. It is excellent for primitive style hooking and the strips can become rather uneven and not so perfect.

1. Tear the wool into ½" strips.

2. Use a sharp pair of scissors to cut each strip in half lengthwise.

Method 2

This method utilizes a special ruler and mat designed specifically for rug hooking plus a rotary cutter. The mat is designed especially for cutting strips in two measurements: #8 or ¼" strips, as well as #6 strips (also known as ¹/₃₂ cut). Keep in mind that cutting wool strips narrower than ¼" is not easy and will take practice and patience.

1. Place the fabric piece on the mat at the desired width.

2. Use the rotary cutter to slice the strip to the desired width.

Cutting by Machine

The quickest method of cutting wool strips is to use a mechanical wool-stripping machine. Once you have decided that rug hooking is really for you, the investment in one of these machines is a wise decision. Wool stripping machines can cut your strips accurately and quickly with little effort. There are several models available (see Resources, page 128). Each of these wool-stripping machines offers a variety of different-sized blades that allow you to cut different-sized strips, anywhere from a #4 to a #10 cut. On most blades, you are able to cut more than one strip at a time, depending on the size.

All of the rugs created in this book were hooked in a #8 or #8.5 cut. Periodically, a #6 cut was used for smaller details or outlining and is noted in each of the patterns. For special details, such as eyes or noses, you might even want smaller strips. A special blade in a smaller cut makes this easy. Also keep in mind on small detailed areas that you can hook the area with narrow yarn or even one to two strands of perle cotton thread.

Use the chart here as a guide for strip sizes. The size of a strip is referred to by a number that represents ¹/₃₂" increments. For example, a #8 cut can also be referred to as an ⁸/₃₂" or ¹/₄" strip. A #6 cut is referred to as a ⁶/₃₂" or ³/₁₆" strip. This mathematical system holds true until the #8.5 strip, which is actually a ¹⁰/₃₂" or ⁵/₁₆". The #9 is a ³/₈" cut and a #10 is a ¹/₂" cut.

Strip Size Guide

#2 ²/₃₂"

#3 ³/₃₂"

#4 ⁴/₃₂" or ¹/₈"

#5 ⁵/₃₂"

#6 ⁶/₃₂" or ³/₁₆"

#7 ⁷/₃₂"

#8 ⁸/₃₂" or ¹/₄"

#8.5 ¹⁰/₃₂" or ⁵/₁₆"

#9 ¹²/₃₂" or ³/₈"

#10 ¹⁶/₃₂" or ¹/₂"

There are two different types of mechanical cutters: clamp-on and tabletop. Both types work well for rug hooking and it is a personal choice as to which you decide to use. Clamp-on strippers have a clamping device that attaches to the edge of a table or other sturdy surface. Tabletop cutters have strong suction cups on the bottom that can be suctioned onto most hard surfaces. The biggest difference between the two types of cutters is in the handles. The handles on clamp-on cutters have a larger revolution, meaning you will not have to crank the handle as many times to cut your strips. Tabletop models have a smaller revolution, so you will be turning the handle around more times to cut your strips. Clamp-on strippers are also more stable, but you will have to find somewhere to clamp them down.

Tara's Tip: I prefer the clamp-on model. When I first purchased it, I placed a piece of old towel on the edge of my table and then clamped the stripper onto the edge of my table. Over time, I discovered a resource for a movable cutter stand. These wood stands are small, lightweight and designed to hold your clamp-on model cutters to perfection. See Resources, page 128, for information on the cutter stand.

Each stripper comes with one blade, and the size choice is yours. You may also purchase additional stripper blades in a variety of sizes for each of the cutters available. It is easy to change stripper blades.

There are currently three different brands of clamp-on strippers on the market: the Bliss, Fraser and the Townsend. Each brand of stripper has its own perks and qualities and before investing in one, research each. If you know other rug hookers, ask to use their machines to see if you like them. Most rug-hooking shops and several quilt shops also have cloth-stripping machines that customers can use.

Transferring Patterns to Cloth

Once you have chosen the perfect hooking pattern, the pattern needs to be transferred onto the foundation fabric.

To transfer from paper to red dot fabric:

1. Find the finished size of the project. This information is necessary, regardless of the pattern you are hooking.

2. Cut a piece of foundation fabric at least 4" wider on each side than the finished size dimensions of the pattern. For example, if the finished size is 10" x 14", cut a piece of foundation fabric that measures 18" x 22". The excess backing ensures that pattern will fit comfortably into your hoop or onto your gripper frame with plenty of room to work.

3. Serge or double-zigzag stitch the outer edges of the foundation fabric to prevent them from fraying and unraveling. If you do not have a serger or sewing machine, simply cover the edges of the foundation fabric with a wide masking tape. Place half of the width of tape on the top edge of the foundation fabric and fold the opposite half of the tape onto the backside. Eventually either the stitched or taped edges will be cut off and discarded.

4. Enlarge the chosen design to the correct finished size, if needed, by taking it to your local copy shop. (All of the patterns in this book are already full-size, so this step will not be needed for any of them.)

5. Tape the full-size pattern right-side up on a hard, flat surface. Be sure that the surface you are using is larger than the pattern so that you will not have to shift the pattern around.

6. Pin or tape down a piece of red dot transfer fabric on top of the pattern to hold in place. Be sure your red dot fabric is slightly larger than the pattern that will be traced and that the fabric is laying straight on top of your pattern. The tiny red dots on the fabric will make it easier for you to draw or trace straight lines, so make sure the red dot lays accordingly over your pattern.

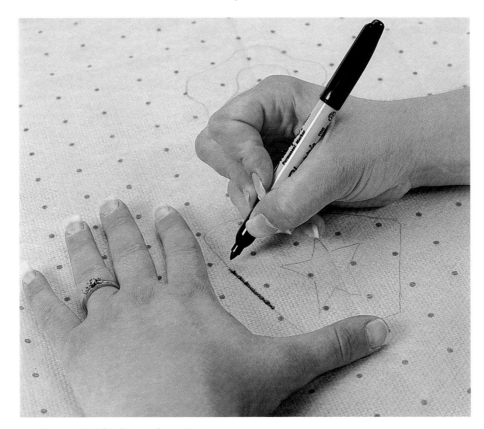

Place red dot fabric over the pattern.

7. Use a pencil or pen to trace the center of the design onto the red dot fabric. Work from the inside to the outside of the pattern so you do not smear the pencil lead or pen ink while drawing. Take your time while tracing the design and use a ruler if necessary when tracing straight lines.

8. Double-check to ensure every part of the pattern has been traced and then remove the red dot fabric and the pattern. Set the paper pattern aside.

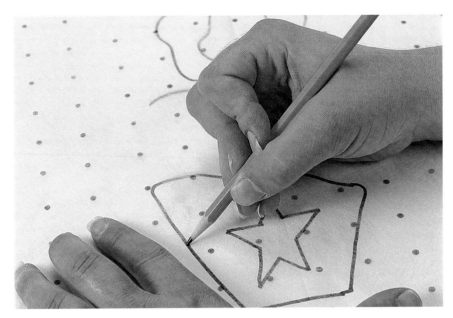
Trace the pattern onto red dot fabric.

To transfer from red dot fabric to foundation fabric:

1. Tape the foundation fabric to a hard, flat surface.

2. Use a black permanent fine point marker to draw your outer finished size dimensions onto the foundation fabric. Be careful to leave the extra 4" of foundation fabric around the outside of the design. If the chosen pattern design also has additional straight borders, those can also be drawn in place here too by following the instructions given in the pattern.

Tara's Tip: In step 2, take great care when drawing your outer borders onto the foundation fabric. Be sure as you are drawing the outer edges of the pattern that you are drawing on the straight of grain. I always take this extra step of drawing my outer edge of the design onto the foundation fabric first, so that I am sure to have the pattern on the straight of grain, which is important when hooking. You don't want crooked edges!

3. Pin the red dot pattern right-side up on top of the foundation fabric, matching the outside pattern edges drawn on the red dot fabric to those drawn on the foundation fabric.

Transfer the pattern from the red dot fabric to the foundation fabric.

4. Use the black permanent marker again, and pressing lightly, trace the interior shapes first and work your way outward on the pattern design. Excess pressure on the marker tip is not necessary and may cause the ink to bleed through the foundation fabric onto the work surface.

Tara's Tip: If red dot transfer fabric is not readily available in your area, you can also use nylon netting or tulle to transfer your designs. Simply transfer your pattern onto the netting or tulle with a black permanent marker. Then lay the netting/tulle on top of your foundation fabric and retrace your drawn lines.

Another easy way to transfer patterns is to use a light box. This works great for smaller-sized hooking patterns. Tape your pattern to the light box and position your foundation fabric over the pattern so that it is laying correctly and straight. Trace your pattern design directly onto the foundation fabric.

Where to Start

To determine where to start hooking on your pattern design, decide what the center of the design is, or the main focal point. On most rug patterns, you will start with the center motif and work your way outward, hooking the main parts of the rug and then later going back and hooking the background followed by the surrounding borders. The following instructions are for a right-handed hooker. If you are left-handed, reverse the directions and hold the wool in the right hand and the hook in the left hand.

Beginning to Hook

If this is your very first time hooking, you may want to simply practice a few loops and rows of hooking on a piece of foundation fabric before starting your pattern. Start with some practice loops, hook a few short rows or even draw a simple circle or flower shape on foundation fabric and play for a little while until you are comfortable with the hook, the frame or hoop and the wool strips.

1. Place your foundation fabric onto your frame or in your hoop, centering the area that you are going to begin hooking first.

If using a hoop, position the foundation fabric over the smaller of the two hoops, lay the larger hoop on top and tighten the bolt.

If using a frame with gripper strips, lay your pattern on top of the gripper strips starting at top of the frame and bring the pattern down and towards you. Holding the pattern in the bottom left and right corners, pull the pattern down taut over the bottom grippers. Tug on the excess foundation fabric around all the sides of the frame. You want the fabric taut in the frame, but not so stretched that your pattern becomes distorted.

2. Hold the hook in your right hand as if it were a pencil.

Place the foundation fabric on the hooking frame.

Tara's Tip: Every rug hook is different and each will require that you hold it differently. Most traditional hookers and teachers will say that you have to hold the hook like you would a pencil, but I have found this difficult with some hooks. Try holding your hook and hooking with it in a variety of different ways.

I am a "jabber" as they call it in the rug-hooking world. I tend to hold my hook with my hand over the handle and jab downward with it into my foundation fabric, or as if I were holding an imaginary pizza cutter.

Regardless of how you hold the hook, the most important thing is the way the tip of the hook is facing. You always want the opening at the tip of the hook facing up. If the opening faces to either side, you will have trouble pulling up your wool loops.

3. Grasp the wool strip that you will begin to hook your pattern with in your left hand between your thumb and forefinger and position your hand beneath the rug hooking pattern, as shown.

Hold the wool strip below the frame.

4. Insert the hook through the hole in the top of the foundation fabric at your starting point.

Insert the hook into the foundation cloth.

5. Place the wool strip in the curve of the hook tip and pull the end of the wool strip up through the hole so that about ½" of the strip shows on the top of the foundation fabric.

Pull the end of the wool strip up through the hole.

Tara's Tip: Always hook inside your black traced lines. By doing so, the pattern will be hooked in the correct size. If you were to hook on the traced line or outside of it, you will be making the pattern larger than it should be and it could throw the design off a bit.

6. Roll your hand to the right as you pull the loop through the foundation fabric on the top of your pattern. (Do the opposite if you are left-handed.) By doing this rolling motion, you are pulling the strip from below the fabric to create your loop instead of taking fabric away from the previously hooked loops.

7. Insert your hook again into the very next hole where your ½" tail came through the foundation fabric.

8. Catch the wool strip in the curve of the hook tip and pull up a loop. You can use your fingers underneath to help guide the wool strip onto your hook correctly. Loops should traditionally be as high as they are wide. In other words, if you are hooking with a #8 or ¼" strip of wool, your goal is to have the loops a ¼" high from the foundation fabric.

Tara's Tip: Do not let the height of your loops overpower you right now. Over time, you will begin to have your own hooking rhythm and your loops will eventually be all the same, uniform height throughout your rugs. For now, simply focus on pulling the loops up correctly and not having them twisting and turning. A nice fluffy loop is what you are looking for—no twisted loops.

9. Continue hooking by inserting the hook into every second or third hole. The loops should only be touching each other and not crammed together. If you over-pack your loops, the rug will pucker and curl, which is very difficult to flatten out when the rug is finished without ripping the entire section apart.

Continue to pull loops up on the pattern.

10. When you come to the end of the wool strip, pull the tail of the strip up in the very next hole from your last loop so that you have at least a ½" tail.

11. Begin hooking another strip by inserting the tip of the hook into the same hole where the previous strip ended. Pull up the beginning of the strip so that a ½" tail is showing, as shown.

End a strip of wool and begin a new one.

Tara's Tip: Never start or stop hooking in a corner. You always want to begin or end your wool strips away from any corners. Corners of hooked rugs are stress points and stopping or starting in those areas will only result in a rug in need of repair over time.

12. Continue hooking in every second or third hole. Be sure that you stagger your stopping and starting points from row to row. You never want these points to stack on top of each other, as this will create a weak spot in the rug that can be an eyesore.

Tara's Tip: Never drag a strip of wool from one spot to another on the backside of the rug. Always stop hooking, clip the ends and start hooking again in the new area, even if the places are only a few holes away. Crossovers, lumps, bumps and twists on the backside of a hooked rug are a big no-no and if they are allowed to happen, the rug will take an extra beating when those areas are walked on and they will wear away, causing a rug to need repair. The backside of a rug should be flat with no bumps!

13. Remember to clip the tails off at the same height as your loops from time to time.

14. Continue to hook until all of your center motifs are completely hooked.

15. Begin hooking your background colors by hooking one to two rows of background color around each of the shapes.

Tara's Tip: Remember that it is OK to turn your frame or hoop as you work. Generally, you want to hook from right to left if you are right-handed and the opposite if you are left-handed. When you are working on circles, stars or coming to a corner, you are much better off turning the frame to meet your needs rather than trying to make yourself uncomfortable while hooking. With this said, remember that all rules can be broken. If you find it uncomfortable to hook from right to left, then find a way that is more comfortable for you. Hook from top to bottom if it feels right. The key is to do what feels right and what works best for you.

16. Continue to fill in the background area, until you are 1" to 2" away from the drawn border edge or the outside edge of the rug.

17. Hook one to two straight rows, following this drawn line. Once the straight outside background edges are hooked, continue to fill in the background area.

Tara's Tip: Remember not to pack your loops. Your finished rug will not lie flat if the wool loops are packed in your rug. Crowding loops is a common problem for beginners. On the top of the rug, the loops should only be touching each other. On the back of the rug, some backing should show between each of the rows. Be sure to check the back of your rug every once in a while for large white areas or windows of unhooked foundation fabric, and then go back and hook these areas if they are found.

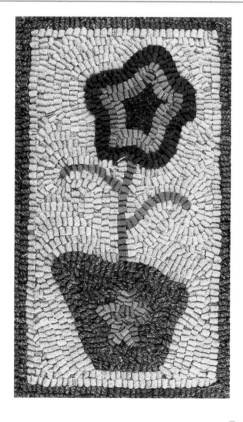

Hooking Techniques

Hooking Corners

The easiest way to hook a corner is to hook towards you. When you reach the corner, turn the frame clockwise and continue to hook towards you. By turning your frame when you reach the corner point, you automatically change the direction of your hooking and your hands will naturally guide the wool strip the way it needs to go. Just remember to never start or stop a wool strip in a corner. Begin or end the strip a few holes before or after the corner.

Hooking Circles

When hooking circles, be sure to hook from the outside to the inside of the circle. Begin just inside the drawn line of your pattern and hook as you normally would, turning the

frame every few loops. When you complete the first outside row of the circle, go on to the next row just inside the last. Continue hooking in this manner until the circle is complete. Remember to turn your frame as needed and your hands will automatically guide the wool strips in the direction they need to go and the hook will do the rest.

Hooking Stars

When hooking stars, the method is the same as if you were hooking a corner. Hook the basic shape correctly and the rest will fall into place. For a sharp, pointed-looking star, hook inside the drawn pattern line and when you get to a point, turn your frame clockwise, hook exactly on the drawn pattern line point, turn your frame again and continue to hook inside the pattern line down the opposite side.

Hooking 'S' Patterns

A fun addition to any background or large motif is to add some direction and punch to the area. This is especially helpful to add movement to large areas of background hooking. You can either hook random "S" shapes while hooking, just allowing yourself free range of the area, or use your permanent marker to draw an "S" pattern in the area to be hooked so that you have a pattern to follow.

Begin by hooking as you normally would, following the pattern line drawn or simply hooking in curvy lines. Continue to follow this direction for the surrounding rows.

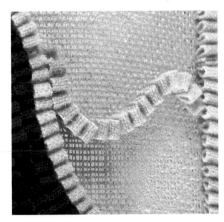

An "S" pattern hooked in the background helps give the finished piece movement.

Crazy Patch Hooking

The Folk Art Cat rug, shown here and detailed on pages 94-96, incorporates a crazy patch hooking background.

This method mimics an old crazy patch quilt style. The key to this style of hooking is in your color choices. Choose colors that will work well together in a background setting and ones that will also help offset your center motif. You have the choice of just randomly hooking square, circular or triangular shapes into your backgrounds. Odd shapes also work well and add dimension to your rug. It can be helpful to use your black permanent marker and draw a few shapes on the background of your pattern so that you have a guide to follow.

Reverse Hooking

Reverse hooking is an excellent way to make letters or certain areas of your rug stand out more if they have become lost in the design. It is also a way to correct colors that are just not working in your rug, but before you go and reverse hook an area, continue hooking other areas of the rug and come back to the problem area later. Often, as you work in other areas, you will find that what you thought was a problem, now works.

Reverse hooking is simply removing or ripping the wool strips out that are not working and then re-hooking the area again. To "reverse hook" or remove some of the loops already hooked, simply insert the point of your hook into the loop you want to remove and gently pull upward.

Initials or Dates

Bouquet of Love Rug, shown here and detailed on pages 84 and 85, contains initials in the lower corner.

Another fun addition to any hooked rug is putting your initials or the year the rug was completed into the background area. Simply draw the letters for your initials or the year onto the foundation fabric of your rug prior to hooking the area where you want them. Hook as you normally would, using a color that will stand out in the rug, yet will still work well with the other chosen colors.

Hooking in Rows

The Flag Footstool design, shown here and detailed on pages 110-112, was best accomplished hooking in rows.

Sometimes, hooking the entire design in straight rows will work out better than trying to add curves and other shapes to the hooking. A flag or smaller design works better when hooked in straight rows so that you don't lose the overall design itself. If you were to hook a larger flag that would offer you more room for each of the strips, it would be easier to fit in nice curvy rows and shapes.

Borders

A variety of borders.

Borders can add a lot of life to a hooked rug, whether they are simple or extravagant. Some borders are as easy as a few straight rows of hooking. Others have designs and shapes built into them. If you are hooking a border that is made up of simple rows, continue hooking and following the shape of the outside edges of the background color of the rug.

If your border has a design in it, hook the design first. Then hook your last outside row and fill the rest of the border in.

Tara's Tip: Remember to use colors that are already in your rug design or that work well and blend with your design in your border. Never introduce new colors that pop out at you in the border area, this will only draw attention to the border and take away from the design.

Chapter 5

Finishing and Aftercare

There are several different ways to finish the edges of your hooked rug. Read through this chapter completely before hooking the outside edges of your hooked rug design. Choose a way to finish your rug that will work best for you and still add beauty and durability to the outside finished edges.

Binding Tape

The binding tape most rug hookers use is 1¼"- to 1½"-wide 100 percent cotton tape. Try to match the color of the binding tape to the color of the last row of hooking. If the color cannot be matched exactly, use the next closest shade.

To determine how much binding tape you will need, measure the outside perimeter of your rug and add 12". This additional 12" will allow for shrinkage when you pre-wash your binding tape. Some colors of binding tape will bleed excess dyes onto your rug, so be sure to pre-wash in a normal wash cycle in your washing machine and dry.

Binding tape can be attached before hooking your rug or after. If you choose to attach the binding tape before hooking the rug, remember the rug size cannot be changed or enlarged once the tape is sewn in place.

Cotton binding tape finishes a rug with a clean edge.

To attach binding tape by hand:

1. Serge or double-zigzag stitch ½" to ¾" away from the edge of the hooked rug. Trim off excess foundation fabric if you have zigzagged the edge. Choose a starting point that is not near a corner.

2. Place the binding tape on top of the rug along the outermost edge with the right side of the binding tape facing the right side of the hooked rug. Shift the binding tape so that approximately ¼" of the tape is now laying on the foundation fabric and pin in place. The majority of the width of the binding tape should be on the hooked rug, not on the excess foundation fabric.

3. Use a strong double-thread in the needle to stitch by hand the outermost lengthwise edge of the binding tape to the excess foundation fabric around the entire hooked rug.

To attach binding tape by machine:

Sewing binding tape on by hand after the hooking is completed does tire your fingers out. Binding tape can be machine-stitched in place using a medium stitch length before hooking if you are going to hook on monk's cloth or linen foundation fabric. If you are hooking on burlap, however, you need to handstitch the binding in place using small ¼" stitches and strong thread.

1. Place the binding tape on the outside drawn line of the pattern with the right side of the binding tape facing and laying on the right side of the pattern.

2. Machine-stitch as close to the drawn pattern edge as possible, using a scant ⅛" seam allowance. Be sure to stitch slowly and keep your stitching lines on the straight of grain on the foundation fabric. Ease the tape around the corners.

3. Once you come back to your starting point, fold the binding tape under ½" and lay it directly on top of the previously stitched beginning piece of binding tape.

4. Stitch in place and be sure to take a couple of backstitches to stabilize.

5. Hook the outside rows as close as possible to the binding tape when you get to this point in your hooking.

Tara's Tip: To hold the binding tape out of the way while hooking the outside edges, simply use sewing pins or T-pins to tack it down on the excess foundation fabric.

To finish the binding edge:

Regardless of how the binding tape was attached, use this method to finish the edge.

1. Fold the binding to the wrong side of the rug.

2. Hand-sew the outer edge of the binding tape to the rug with doubled, heavy-duty thread. Be sure to start attaching the binding tape to the rug in an area that is away from the corners and catch only a thread or two of the foundation fabric in each of your stitches. Use a whipstitch, blind-stitch or overcast stitch to secure the binding in place.

3. When you come near a corner, stop stitching and prepare the mitered corner so that everything will lay smooth and flat. Sneak your fingers into the corner area under the binding tape and adjust the foundation fabric so that it is laying flat and smooth in a nice mitered fashion. For the binding, do the same so the corners are nicely mitered. Stitch the mitered corners down.

4. When you reach the beginning point, continue stitching the binding tape down through the folded layer of binding tape to create a nice flat surface.

Wool Cording Edge

You will need a sewing machine to create the wool strip that is wrapped around a piece of cotton cording that will be used as binding. It is easy to do and it protects the edges of the rug in the best way possible. By using a simple piece of ¼" to ⅜" cording inside a sleeve of wool for the outside edges, you create a nice "bumper" for the edges of your hooked rug. (The size of the cording used is determined by the height of your loops. If you hook ¼" high, purchase ¼" 100 percent cotton cording, and so on.) This finish will give a lot more life to your rug, helping to prevent wear on the hooked loops around the perimeter.

1. Serge or double-zigzag stitch the edge of the rug approximately ¾" to 1" away from the finished hooked edge, as shown at right. Cut off the excess foundation fabric if you have zigzag stitched.

2. Measure the perimeter around the rug and add 8" to 10" extra to that measurement. For example, on a rug that is 6" square, perimeter around the rug is 24" plus an additional 8" to 10".

3. Cut a piece of cotton cording the length determined in step 2. Taping the cording with a tiny piece of tape wrapped around the cording before cutting will prevent it from fraying.

4. Tear a piece of 100 percent wool fabric that has already been washed and dried into a 2½"-wide strip, as shown below right.

Tara's Tip: To prevent many seams in your wool binding strips, use a length of fabric that will be long enough to go around the rug. For example, if you were to use a lot of black or brown for binding edges, cut a piece of wool that is 2, 4 or 6 yards or longer and keep this wool just for binding. Tear the 2½"-wide strip along the length and you will have one continuous strip of binding wool. If you do need to seam pieces of wool together, be sure to stitch them together on the diagonal so that the seams will not be lying on top of each other in your binding.

Zigzag the edge of the rug.

Use cotton cording and a 2½"-wide wool strip.

5. Attach the zipper foot or the cording foot to your sewing machine.

6. Lay the long wool strip with the wrong side up with the cotton cording on top near the left edge of the wool strip.

7. Wrap the left lengthwise edge of the strip over the cording. Do not match the long edges of the wool strip. Let the side of the wool strip that is on top of the cording, extend approximately one-third of the way down the wool strip. This will give your wool cording a short and a long seam allowance.

8. Pin the two layers of wool together to hold them together while stitching.

9. Place the wool and cording under the zipper foot along the edge of the cording as close as you can get it, as shown below.

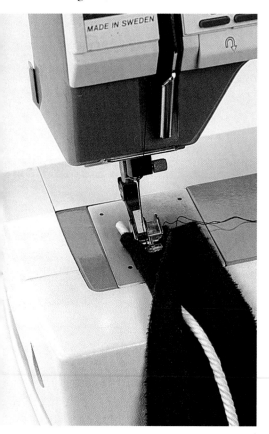

Place cording and wool strip in the sewing machine.

10. Stitch the entire length of the wool cording, as shown below.

Stitch the length of wool with cording inside.

11. With the rug right side up, place the wool binding face down on top with the corded edge towards the rug and the shorter seam allowance facing the excess foundation fabric. Place the start of the wool binding away from any corners.

12. Use heavy-duty thread that matches the color of the wool binding and doubled on the needle to hand-stitch 1" to 2" from the beginning edge of the binding. Insert the needle into the foundation fabric from the back of the rug, being careful not to catch the long-edged seam allowance on the wool binding. Stitch as close as you possibly can to the hooked edge. (You don't want any backing showing once the binding is stitched in place.)

13. Pull the needle and thread to the top of the rug, as shown, checking your work to be sure the stitching is right next to the hooked edge.

Pull the needle and thread to the top of the rug.

14. Move a scant ¼" forward, pull the needle and thread through the wool binding between the straight stitches and the cording, and reinsert the needle into the foundation fabric with the needle exiting back through a few threads of the foundation fabric near the hooked rug edge on the top of the design, as shown in the photo below.

Tara's Tip: Pay close attention while stitching the wool binding in place and be careful not to catch the cotton fibers of the cording that is inside the binding.

Exit the back of the rug as you stitch.

15. Continue stitching around the rug in this same fashion until you are about 2" away from the beginning of the opposite end of the wool binding.

16. Trim the excess away from the free edge, so that the remaining wool overlaps each other by at least 1", as shown below. It may also be necessary to trim the ends of the cotton cording so that they butt together.

Trim ends on wool binding strip where the raw edges meet.

17. Continue to stitch the wool binding edge to the rug with the wool strip ends overlapping each other and the ends of the cording butted together.

Tara's Tip: *When you come near a corner when attaching wool binding, simply start taking smaller and closer stitches in the corner area. It also helps to push a little extra cording into the corner area to offer a little more give instead of the cording rolling forward.*

18. Double-thread the needle again with heavy duty thread and hand-stitch the loose, wider seam allowance to the underside of the rug. This seam allowance should cover up the entire edge of the excess foundation fabric. You want this wide seam allowance to lay flat and smooth against the back of the rug, so do not pull the seam allowance back too tightly.

19. Take small stitches by hand (whipstitch, blind-stitch or overcast stitch) into the foundation fabric and the binding edge, as shown. Miter the corners as you stitch.

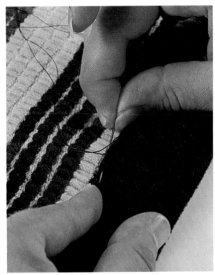

Hand-stitch the wider seam allowance to the back of the hooked rug.

Tara's Tip: *Pay close attention when stitching the binding edge onto your rug. Be sure to only pick up one to two threads of the foundation fabric and reinsert the needle into the wool binding edge. Never stitch into any of the hooked loops.*

20. When you come back to your beginning, be sure the wool edges are overlapping each other and stitch down on the hooked rug, as shown below.

Finish the stitching.

The finished back side of the hooked rug bound with wool binding.

Whipstitching the Edges

Whipstitching the edges of your rug will take a bit more time, but the end result is beautiful with its professional-looking clean finish. It is also the preferred method for round and oval rugs, as it helps to prevent the puckering that can result when binding with wool cording.

When whipping the edges of your rug, try one of several different 100 percent wool yarns available on the market today. Three-ply wool yarn that is a bit more bulky seems to work best.

Paternayan, a Persian wool yarn that is also a three-ply yarn, is a bit thinner, but the availability of colors is fabulous. Many yarns can be found at your local rug hooking, needlepoint and knitting shops. (See Resources, page 128, for additional options.)

When purchasing wool yarn, figure a 12" length of yarn will cover approximately 1" of space on the rug edge. This measurement is figured with a thicker or bulkier yarn in mind. If you choose a thinner yarn, estimate on the high side for the amount of yarn needed. Measure the perimeter of your rug and add an additional 2 to 4 yards in length of yarn needed to be sure you have enough to cover the edge.

1. Serge or double-zigzag stitch about ¾" to 1" away from the outermost hooked edge. The distance between the last row of hooking and the stitching depends upon the width of cording. After cutting off the excess foundation fabric, you need to be able to roll the remaining foundation fabric over and around your cotton cording so that it is completely covered, with no excess.

2. Place the cording on the edge of the foundation fabric and roll the cording inside with the right side of the rug facing up. Once rolled, the cording should lay right next to the last hooked row.

3. Use a tapestry needle that is double-threaded with heavy duty thread and whipstitch or overcast stitch the backing around the cording with stitches approximately ¼" apart, as shown at right. Be sure you are inserting your needle into the foundation fabric and not into any wool loops. Stitch as close to the outside row of hooking as possible.

4. Continue stitching around the perimeter of the rug. Before making the last few stitches when back to the beginning point, cut off any excess cording so that the edges will butt nicely together and lay flat.

5. Use a tapestry or gold needle with a large eye opening and thread it with 1 yard of wool yarn. Using a length of yarn that is longer than 36" can cause the wool yarn to twist and knot up as you whip your edges.

6. Lay the last 1" of the yarn on top of the foundation fabric on the front side of the rug, near the last row of hooking and hold it in place with your fingers. This is where you will begin to whipstitch the rug edges, so be sure you are nowhere near a corner.

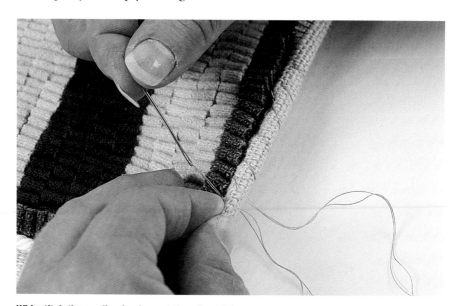

Whipstitch the cording in place at the edge of the rug.

7. Insert the needle into the foundation fabric, entering through the front of the fabric and exiting out the back, as close as possible to the last row of hooking, as shown below (top left photo). Pull the yarn all the way through, stopping when 1" of yarn remains on the top of your rug.

8. Bring the needle to the front of the rug by pulling the yarn up and over the outer corded edge.

9. Insert the needle back into the foundation fabric in the hole directly next to where you began, as close as possible to your last row of hooking, as shown below (top right photo).

10. Pull the needle and yarn through to the back of the rug again, making sure that you are hiding the beginning tail of yarn underneath the yarn loops (top right).

Tara's Tip: When whipping the edge of your rug, be sure to keep the tension on the yarn even as you are pulling it through the foundation fabric. Also be careful not to catch the fibers from the cotton cording in your stitches. Work either from left to right or right to left when whipping the edges with yarn. Choose one direction to stitch in and stay with it; do not change halfway through.

11. When you have about 3" of yarn remaining, bury the yarn by pulling the needle through the previous yarn stitches and then cut off the yarn end, as shown (bottom left).

12. When nearing a corner, be sure you have enough yarn loaded on the needle to make it completely around the corner. Whipstitch up to the corner, keeping your stitches even, and once you reach the point of a corner, make two or three stitches in each hole to completely cover the edge. Keep the tension on the yarn even. If you over-pull the yarn, it will cause the corner to curl up. Once you have made it around the corner, continue whipping the edges in the normal manner.

13. Bury the thread as usual and cut off the excess yarn when the entire edge is finished, as shown below (bottom right photo).

Begin to whipstitch the edge.

Continue to whipstitch with the needle properly inserted.

End a piece of yarn by burying the yarn in previous stitches.

The finished whipstitched edge of the Barn Star rug, shown here and detailed on pages 92 and 93.

Blocking the Rug

After a rug is finished, it needs to be set with heat and steam, which is what blocking is. Blocking a finished rug is an important final step in completing your rug, as it helps the loops look more uniform (even when they are slightly different heights). Blocking also helps to ensure the edges of the rug are and stay the way you intended them—straight or completely round if on a round rug. Blocking can further help hide some minor bubbles in your rug.

Blocking is done after you have stitched your binding in place generally, but if you prefer to block your rug prior to finishing the edges, that is OK too. Just be sure to trim off and serge or double-zigzag stitch the outside edges so they are not in the way. Actually, blocking also can be done after the rug has been in storage or in use for a time to give it a little more fresh appearance.

1. Place a bath towel (preferably one that is larger than your hooked piece) on a hard, flat surface.

2. Place the rug wrong-side up on top of the towel.

3. Wet a second towel that is also larger, if possible, than your rug. Wring the excess water from the towel and place it on top of the hooked rug.

4. Set an iron on a medium to high heat setting.

5. Place the iron in the center of the rug on top of the wet towel and stamp-press the area, as shown. Do not use an ironing motion. Hold the iron in place for a few seconds until you see steam rising from the towel. Lift the iron and stamp-press again, working in an outward circular motion from the center of the rug design, as shown below. Continue on in this manner until you have covered the complete surface of the rug.

6. Remove the top towel and turn the rug right-side up.

7. Place the wet towel back on top of the rug and repeat the blocking steps again until you have completely covered the entire rug.

8. Remove the top towel and allow the rug to dry overnight (or until completely dry) without moving it.

Stamp-press the rug with an iron.

Care and Cleaning

Hooked rugs are simple to take care of and there is nothing special needed for their care. If your rugs are going to be used on the floor, a simple cleaning everyday with a handheld or a standard vacuum with the beater bars turned off is all that is needed.

If a spill occurs on your rug, clean it up as soon as possible.

1. Add some water to a bucket and pour in a generous amount of dishwashing detergent, such as Ivory dish soap.

2. Swish the water around to create a lot of suds.

3. Dip a dry sponge into the suds only, not the water.

4. Dab the suds-filled sponge onto the area of the rug you wish to clean and rub gently. The suds will remain on the surface of the rug and will not set in.

5. Allow the rug to dry in a well-ventilated area and vacuum, if needed, with the beater bars turned off on the machine. (This method also works well if you just need to brighten up a dingy-looking rug.)

Another method for cleaning follows in the footsteps of how our ancestors took care of rugs. Simply take the rugs outdoors and give them a good shake or two. Allow the rugs to hang over the edge of a deck or fence, out of direct sunlight, to freshen them. Only shake rugs made on linen or monk's cloth. Burlap fibers are not strong enough to be shaken.

If you are lucky enough to have a vintage or antique rug, never shake them or use a vacuum on them. Always seek out the advice of a professional who is educated in the repair and care of old rugs.

Storing Rugs

When you need to store your rugs, always roll them up and never fold them. Simply roll your hand-hooked rugs into a tube with the right side of the rug facing outward. The rugs can be stacked on top of each other with ease.

If you have the room to store your rugs flat, feel free to do so. Just be certain they are flat and have no corners folded under.

Chapter 6

Projects

At last, the moment you have worked toward—finding the perfect project to hook for your home or as a special gift. Enjoy the projects included in this chapter.

The rug projects in this book were designed to be simple, yet fun. If you are new to rug hooking, go back and read the introductory chapters before beginning any rug-hooking project.

All of the rug projects here have been hooked in either a #8 or #8.5 cut, with a #6 cut used in some of the projects for accents or highlights. Each of the projects will tell you the cut used, but you can hook them in whatever size strip desired. If you hook the projects in a size strip that is different than what is listed, however, the amounts of wool needed for the project may change.

The quantity of wool needed for each project is listed either by yardage or by size. If several different shades of one color are needed, the total amount of wool needed will be shown. Calculating yardage is not difficult, but it is never exact. Everyone hooks at different heights and everyone will have differing amounts of waste. The yardage calculations are based on wool that has been washed and dried (felted). The felted wool measurements are based on wool that is 54" wide,

which is an average width of wool once it is washed and dried.

If you need to recalculate wool for any of the projects in this book or in the future, remember to measure the area to be hooked and multiply those numbers to come up with the square inches. Then take the square inches and multiply by 4 if you have been hooking for a while or if you hook an average height compared to your wool strip width. Multiply by 5 if you are a beginning hooker or if you hook on the high side. For example, if the area to be hooked measures 2" square, multiply the width by the height (2" x 2") for 4 square inches. Take 4 and multiply it by either 4 or 5 and this will be the total square inches of wool needed to hook that particular area (either 16" or 20").

When purchasing hand-dyed wool or dyeing your own, be sure to buy or dye more than you think you will need. Every dye lot of wool differs from dye pot to dye pot, so you are safer if you just have extra on hand.

Feel free to change the designs to suit your own needs and change the colors as you see fit. Make it your own.

Basic Directions for Each Project

1. Prepare the foundation fabric, as discussed in Chapter 4, pages 47 and 48.
2. Draw the outside dimensions for the pattern onto the foundation fabric. Also draw any borders that are simple straight lines.
3. Transfer the pattern design onto the foundation fabric.
4. Decide on how you will bind the edges of your rug. Remember, if you choose to attach the cotton binding tape around the edge before hooking your rug, it needs to happen first.
5. Cut wool strips in the desired size for hooking. Never cut all the wool at once, begin with a small amount of wool strips and cut more as needed.

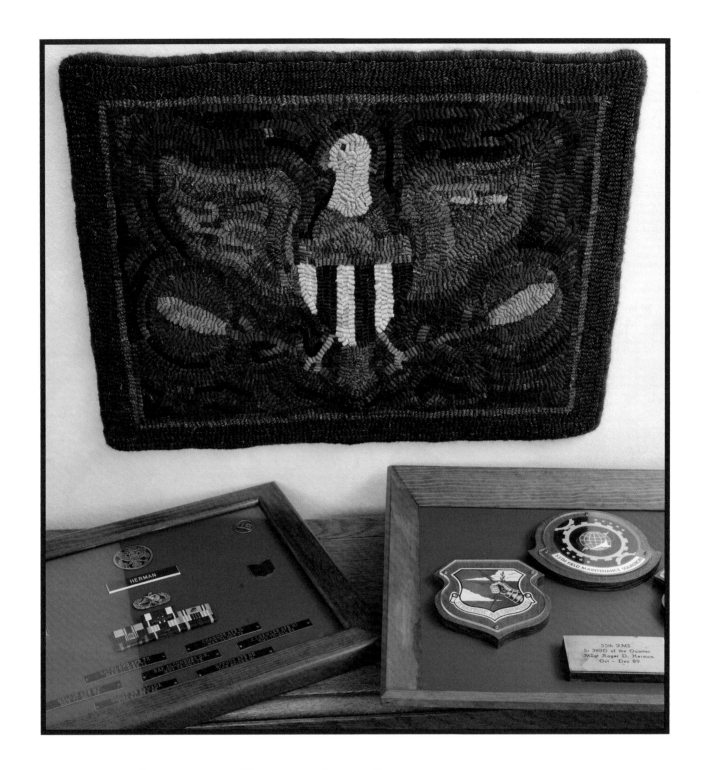

American Symbol

The bald eagle is the symbol for the United States of America. The colors of the flag are shown in the shield and the eagle holds simple primitive pomegranates in its claws. Pomegranates are known as a delicious fruit as well as for their medicinal healing powers. This rug was designed to reflect my belief that the USA will heal over time from the disasters that occurred on Sept. 11, 2001.

Materials

(Yardage based on 54"-wide wool fabrics and using #8 and #6 cut wool strips.)

25" x 32" foundation fabric

¾-yard dark antique black wool (background)

⅓-yard dark brown plaid wool (outer border)

¼-yard variety of browns (eagle)

⅛-yard gold wool (beak and pomegranates)

⅛-yard orange wool (pomegranate)

⅛-yard tan/cream wool (eagle head)

⅛-yard dark brown wool (outline on eagle)

⅛-yard tan wool (inner border)

⅛-yard red wool (flag)

⅛-yard blue wool (upper area of shield)

⅛-yard off-white wool (flag)

1/16-yard green wool (pomegranate stems)

1/16-yard outline fabric* (pomegranates)

1 yard red dot tracer fabric

Fine-point permanent black marker

Pen or pencil

38 yards 100% wool yarn or ¼-yard wool (binding rug edges)

American Symbol pattern

*Used for this project: a blue plaid and #6 cut strips.

Planning for this Project

Finished size: 17" x 24"

The background color used for this rug is the Primitive Black recipe provided on page 40. Natural, gray, tan and several plaids and tweeds were over-dyed to achieve the antique-looking background you see.

To give the eagle a very primitive look, 12 different shades of rusty brown wools were used, including an assortment of hand-dyed, recycled and as-is plaids and tweeds.

Remember when selecting your background and border colors to choose shades that work together. This rug has a warm feeling to the shades of black. The warm shades of border wools work with— not against—the colors already in the rug.

Hooking the Rug

1. Use the marker to draw a 17" x 24" rectangle centered on the foundation fabric. Draw another rectangle 1" inside the first to mark the outer border area and a third rectangle ¼" inside the second for the inner border, as shown in Figure 6-1.

2. Use a pencil or pen to trace the full-size American Symbol pattern from the pullout pattern sheet onto the red dot tracer fabric.

3. Use the marker to transfer the pattern onto the foundation fabric, centering the design in the innermost rectangle of the pattern, as in Figure 6-2.

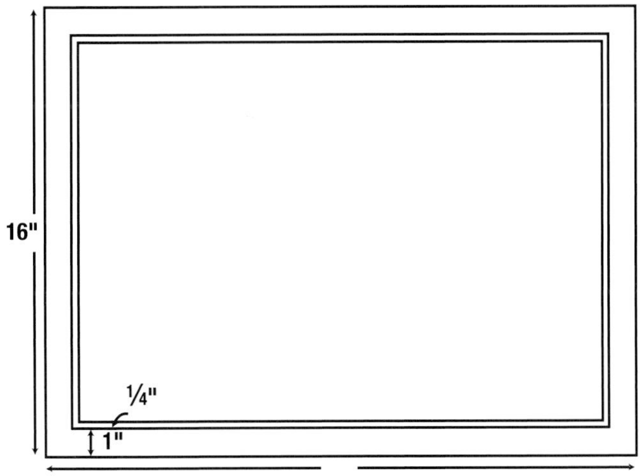

16"

¼"

1"

Figure 6-1

Figure 6-2

4. Cut the wool strips necessary to begin the project.

5. Hook the design in the following order with the suggested wools (or other wool colors of choice):

- up-and-down stripes on the shield, alternating red and off-white
- upper area of the shield with blue
- eagle's upper chest with assorted browns
- eagle head with the tan/cream-colored wools
- eagle's wings with assorted browns
- eagle's tail with assorted browns
- eagle's claws with gold
- pomegranate stems with green
- pomegranate centers with gold
- pomegranate centers outlined with blue plaid
- pomegranates outlined with blue plaid
- outside portion of the pomegranate with orange wool

6. Outline the eagle design with background wool by hooking one to two rows around the entire shape.

7. Continue hooking the background with dark assorted antique black wools.

8. Hook a single row of loops for the innermost border in tan.

9. Hook the outer border in dark brown plaid.

10. Finish the rug according to the instructions in Chapter 5, choosing one of the binding methods on pages 55-61.

Penny Footstool

*This design, which is reminiscent of a hand-stitched penny rug, provides a great way
to use up fabric scraps in the pennies. This small footstool serves as an accent piece
in my bedroom, but the design also makes for a great mat for your coffee table when
left unmounted.*

Materials

(Yardage based on 54"-wide fabrics and using #8 cut wool strips.)

17" x 19" foundation fabric

1/4-yard primitive black wool (background)

1/3-yard assorted colors wool (pennies or circles)

Small black footstool*

Fine-point permanent black marker

Pen or pencil

1 sheet clear template plastic

Ruler

Clear silicone glue (from local hardware store)

Heavy-duty hook-and-loop tape (optional)

*Used for this project: Wayne Sims Folkart stool (Resources, page 128).

Planning for this Project

Finished size: 9⅛" x 7" x 11"

The "hit-or-miss" or "scrappy-looking" pennies (circles) are a great design to use up leftover wool strips from other projects.

This footstool also would look great with a cream-colored background and the pennies hooked in some nice warm pastel shades. Or try using solid colors of wool for each penny that will coordinate in the room setting in which you will use the footstool.

Hooking the Rug

1. Use the marker to draw an 8⅝" x 10½" rectangle centered on the foundation fabric. The rectangle measurements are sized so that the drawn pattern will be ¼" smaller on every side than the top of the footstool. This ¼" gap is needed so there is room to whip the edges of the rug before placing it on the stool.

Tara's Tip: *Whether you purchase a wood footstool from Wayne Sims Folkart for this project (as in the model), be sure to double-check the measurements of the rectangle drawn in step 1 against the measurements of the top flat edge of the stool.*

2. Use pen or pencil to trace the full-size Figure 6-3: Penny Pattern onto the clear template plastic and cut the pattern out.

Tara's Tip: *As you are hooking the pennies, remember to turn the frame as needed to make hooking easier.*

3. Use the ruler and permanent marker to make small dots from left to right on the top and bottom lines, as in Figure 6-4, in the following increments: 2", 5¼" and 8½".

4. Use the ruler and marker to make small dots from the top down on the right and left side lines, as in Figure 6-4, in the following increments: 2⅞" and 5¾".

5. Use a pencil to connect the dots from the top line of the drawn pattern to the bottom line and from right to left, as shown in Figure 6-5, keeping your pencil lines on grain.

6. Center the circle Penny Pattern on each vertical line and in between each horizontal line, as in Figure 6-6. Remember: This is a primitive-type project and perfection is not required.

7. Cut the wool strips necessary to begin the project.

8. Hook all penny circles in the chosen colors starting at the innermost edge of the drawn pattern and working into the center of each penny.

9. Hook a row of background around the entire outside border edge. Be sure to hook inside the drawn line and not on it.

10. Hook a row of background color around each penny where room permits.

11. Finish hooking in the remaining background.

12. Finish the rug according to the instructions in Chapter 5, choosing one of the binding methods on pages 55-61. (The model has whipstitched edges.) Be sure to block the rug before the next step if planning to adhere it to the top of the stool.

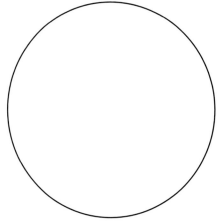

Figure 6-3: Penny Pattern

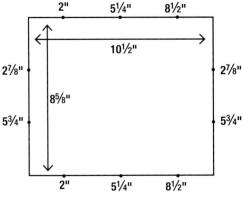

Figure 6-4

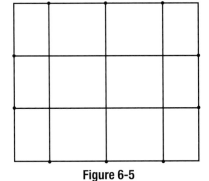

Figure 6-5

Attaching the Stool

1. Wipe the top of the footstool clean to remove any dust or fibers.

2. Apply a thin bead of clear silicone glue ½" in from the outside edge of the stool, as well as a small amount of glue to the center.

3. Center the rug over the top of the footstool and apply pressure. It takes a few minutes before the glue starts to set up, so adjust as needed.

4. Lay a heavy book on top of the rug and stool overnight to apply pressure for a good glue seal.

5. Optional: To make the rug removable from the footstool so you can interchange rugs, use heavy-duty hook-and-loop tape on the rug(s) and stool.

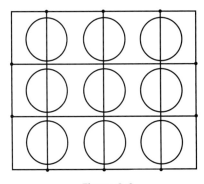

Figure 6-6

Folk Art Horse

So many vintage hooked rugs carry designs of horses that it seemed natural to carry that theme into a more modern design. This rug was hooked in a variety of warm, modern primitive colors. Have fun when hooking the horse. He doesn't have to be black, so try a muted red or a dusty brown as an alternative.

Materials

(Yardage based on 54"-wide wool fabrics and using #8.5 wool strips in the main design and background and #8 cut wool strips for the border.)

28" x 32" foundation fabric

1½ yards assorted color wools (striped inner border)

½-yard assorted primitive black wools (horse and outer border)

½-yard nutmeg-colored wool (background and corners of inner border)

¼-yard assorted color wools (circles in corners of inner border)

1 yard red dot tracer fabric

Fine-point permanent black marker

Pen or pencil

3" square template plastic

Folk Art Horse pattern

Planning for this Project

Finished size: 20" x 24"

The background color for this rug is called nutmeg. It is a warm shade of light rusty brown and works well with the primitive black horse and the hit-or-miss style border.

To give the horse a primitive childlike look, four different wool fabrics (natural, tan and two plaids) were used in the dye pot when dyeing.

Remember when selecting your background colors and your border colors to choose shades that will work together. This rug has a warm feel to the shades of black. The warm shades of border wools work with—not against—the colors already in the rug.

Hooking the Rug

1. Use the marker to draw a 20" x 24" rectangle centered on the foundation fabric. Draw another rectangle 1" inside the first to mark the outer border area and draw a third rectangle 2¾" inside of the second for the innermost border (hit–or–miss style border). Be sure to extend the lines of the innermost rectangle to the outer border edge, as in Figure 6-7, to create the squares needed in the corners of the inner border.

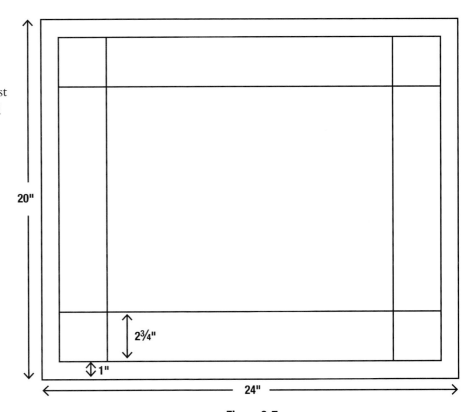

Figure 6-7

2. Use pen or pencil to trace the full-size Circle Pattern (Figure 6-8) onto the clear template plastic and cut the pattern out.

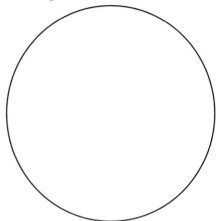

Figure 6-8: Circle Pattern

3. Center a circle in each of the corner squares of the inner border, as in Figure 6-9.

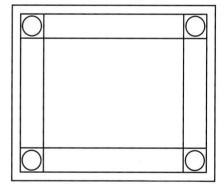

Figure 6-9

4. Use the pen or pencil to trace the full-size Folk Art Horse pattern from the pullout pattern sheet onto the red dot tracer fabric.

5. Use the marker to transfer the pattern onto the foundation fabric, centering the design in the innermost rectangle of the pattern, as in Figure 6-10 at right.

6. Cut the wool strips necessary to begin the project.

7. Hook the horse with primitive black wool.

8. Outline the horse with background wool by hooking one to two rows around the entire shape.

9. Hook one to two rows of background color around the inside of the inner border line.

10. Finish hooking the background.

11. Start in the lower right corner of the inner border and hook the circle inside the square first by following the drawn pattern line. Be sure to hook just inside this line.

12. Outline the square in the inner border with background wool just inside the drawn pattern line.

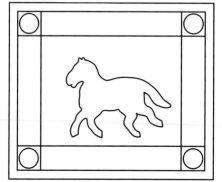

Figure 6-10

13. Finish hooking the corner square of the inner border with the background wool.

Tara's Tip: *When hooking a hit-or-miss type border, make hooking more fun. Place all of your strips for the hit-or-miss border into a large paper bag. Mix the strips around so each time you need a new strip, you reach in and use whichever strip you pull out!*

14. Hook the first row of the inner border in a hit-or-miss fashion with assorted wools, starting right up against the outer edge of background and working downward along the edge of the finished step 13 corner square. Hook down to just inside the drawn pattern line of the outer border.

15. Continue hooking the inner border completely around the rug.

16. Hook the outer border with the leftover primitive black wool from the horse.

17. Finish the rug according to the instructions in Chapter 5, choosing one of the binding methods on pages 55-61.

Plant Pokes

If you love to decorate your home with lots of green plants, but wish for more color, these plant pokes are sure to do just the trick. Hook up a bunch in a variety of colors and you'll soon be adding bursts of color to your home, too.

Materials (for all three combined)

(Yardage based on 54"-wide fabrics and using #8 cut wool strips.)

18" square foundation fabric (enough for all designs)
⅓-yard butter cream dyed wool (background)
⅛-yard red wool (flower)
⅛-yard eggplant wool (flower)
⅛-yard gold wool (flower)
2" x 16" piece brown tweed wool (flower center)
3 18" x ⅜" wooden dowel rods
Fine-point permanent black marker
¼-yard red dot tracer fabric
12-oz. bag Polyfil stuffing
Cool-melt glue gun and glue sticks
Straight pins
Heavy-duty thread (to match background wool)
Hand-sewing needle
Plant Pokes patterns

Planning for this Project

Finished size: 5½"-diameter

These easy-to-hook, round flower designs can easily be made into coasters by binding the edges in a preferred method as detailed in Chapter 5. Another idea is to use these fast and fun plant pokes as great last-minute gifts.

Hooking the Rug

1. Use marker to draw three 5½" round circles on the foundation fabric, leaving a 4" unmarked edge around the outside of each of the drawn circles so the design fits on the frame or hoop.

2. Use pen or pencil to trace the full-size Plant Pokes pattern from the pullout pattern sheet onto the red dot tracer fabric.

3. Use marker to transfer the patterns onto the foundation fabric, centering the design inside each circle.

4. Cut the wool strips necessary to begin the project.

5. Hook each flower in the colors shown (or as desired), referring to the photos below for assistance.

6. Hook a row with background wool strips around the entire outside border edge, staying inside the drawn line and not on it.

7. Hook a row of background color around each flower where room permits.

8. Finish filling in the remaining background area.

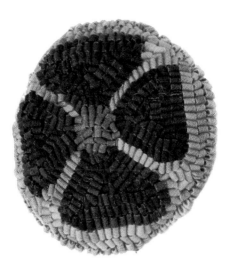  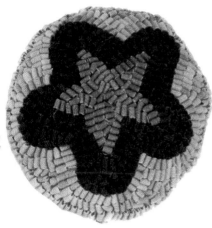

Step 5

Assembling the Pokes

1. Serge or double-zigzag stitch ½" away from the outside edge of each hooked circle.

2. Cut three 6" circles from background wool.

3. Pin a 6" circle on top of each hooked circle with right sides together. The unhooked circles are 6" so there is enough fabric to work with as the smaller hooked pieces are stitched to them. The fullness the loops create will need the extra width for the 6" backing circle.

4. Use a heavy-duty thread doubled on the needle to hand-stitch the two layers together with tiny stitches as close to the hooked edge as possible. Stitch around the circle, leaving a 3" to 4" turn-hole.

5. Turn plant poke heads right-side out and stuff firmly.

6. Insert one dowel into each plant poke head and continue to stuff around the rod.

7. Load the needle again with doubled, heavy-duty thread and stitch the turn-hole nearly closed, leaving a generous ⅛" open.

8. Place a small amount of cool melt glue inside the hole to secure the inside foundation fabric that is near the opening to the dowel rod.

Sheep and Love Boxes

These quick little projects make great gifts for anyone, anytime. The tiny rugs are easy to hook and can be done in a variety of colors to match anyone's décor. The boxes themselves are hinged and can be used to hold a variety of goodies.

Materials (both projects combined)

(Yardage based on 54"-wide fabrics and using #8 cut wool strips.)

16" x 19" foundation fabric (enough for both designs)

⅛-yard medium dusty blue textured wool (sheep background)

⅛-yard pale pink wool (love background)

¹⁄₁₆-yard gray textured wool (sheep body)

2" x 18" strip muted lavender wool (word "Love")

2" x 18" strip black textured wool (sheep head and legs)

2 black 8/0 seed beads (sheep eyes)

2 saltboxes*: one cream and one black

Fine-point permanent black marker

Pen or pencil

¼-yard red dot tracer fabric

20" ⅛"-wide nylon or cotton cording (in colors to match designs)

Clear silicone glue (from local hardware store)

Cool-melt glue gun and glue sticks

Heavy-duty 6" x 8" cardboard

Love Box pattern

Sheep Box pattern

*Used for this project: Wayne Sims Folkart saltboxes (Resources, page 128).

Planning for this Project

Finished size: 3½" x 6"

These tiny hooked rug designs would also look great framed or made into tiny pillows. Enlarge the pattern as needed if you can't find a frame small enough to fit them or simply add more background hooking to the original design.

1. Use marker to draw two 3¼" x 5¾" rectangles on the foundation fabric. Be sure to leave 4" unmarked edge around the outside of each rectangle so each design will fit in the frame or hoop. The rectangle measurements are sized so that the drawn pattern will be a scant ¼" smaller on each side than the front dimensions of the box. This ¼" gap is needed so there is room to whip the edges of the rug before placing it on the box lid.

Tara's Tip: Whether you purchase the wooden boxes from Wayne Sims Folkart for this project (as in the models), be sure to double-check the measurements of the rectangle drawn in step 1 against the measurements of the top flat edge of each box.

2. Use pen or pencil to trace the full-size Sheep Box and Love Box patterns from the pullout pattern sheet onto the red dot tracer fabric.

3. Use the marker to transfer the patterns onto the foundation fabric, centering the design inside each rectangle.

4. Cut the wool strips necessary to begin the project.

5. Hook either the sheep with gray or the word "Love" with lavender (depending on which project).

6. Hook a row around the entire outside border edge with background wool strips (color of wool strips again depends on which design). Be sure to hook inside the drawn line and not on it.

7. Hook a row of background color around either the sheep or "Love," where room permits.

8. Fill in the remaining background.

9. Lay a heavy-duty piece of cardboard on a hard flat surface and place the finished hooked rug on it right-side up.

10. Run a line of clear silicone glue around the perimeter directly next to the last row of hooking on the foundation fabric only and use your finger to smooth the glue outward on the foundation fabric. It is important to completely cover the foundation fabric surrounding the last row of hooking.

11. Allow the project to dry overnight or until completely dry.

12. Use a sharp pair of scissors to cut away all excess foundation fabric so that a scant ⅛" remains on the outside edge of foundation fabric.

Attaching the Boxes

1. Wipe the front of the box clean to remove any dust or fibers and lay the box on its back so the box front is facing upward.

2. Apply a thin line of clear silicone glue ¼" in from the outside edge of the box, as well as in the center of the box. Be careful not to use too much glue, as it could soak through and mar the front of the hooked design.

3. Center the rug over the top of the box, apply pressure and lay a heavy book on top of the rug overnight to seal the glue.

4. Run a thin line of cool melt glue around the outside of the hooked rug design, placing the glue on the foundation fabric as close to the rug edge as possible without getting it on the wool loops. Work in 3" to 4" sections at a time as the cool melt glue will harden and dry pretty quickly.

5. Lay the cording along the perimeter of the rug in the glue line, starting on the bottom edge of the rug and continuing around back to the starting point.

6. Butt the edges of the cording together on the bottom edge of the rug design. Prevent the cording from fraying by laying it in the cool melt glue immediately after it has been cut.

7. Repeat steps 1 through 6 for the remaining box and rug design.

Primitive Floral Rug

Many old rugs had flowers hooked into the design. They were an easy motif to draw and inspiration for the flowers was in abundance. Most flowers in the earlier rugs were simple in design, almost a childlike look to the overall appearance. This rug was partially designed by my youngest daughter, who loves to draw. One day she drew a bunch of flowers for me. Each of the flowers in this rug pattern is her original artwork. Mommy added the leaves and stems.

Materials

(Yardage based on 54"-wide wool fabrics and using #8 cut wool strips)

27" x 32" foundation fabric
1 yard assorted black wools (background)
¼-yard assorted browns and greens (stems and leaves)
⅛-yard red wools (flowers)
⅛-yard gold wools (flowers)
⅛-yard blue wools (flowers)
⅛-yard cream or off-white wools (flowers)
¹⁄₁₆-yard orange wools (flowers)
2" x 16" purple wool (flowers)
Fine-point permanent black marker
1 yard red dot tracer fabric
32 yards 100% wool yarn (binding rug edges)
Primitive Floral pattern

Planning for this Project

Finished size: 19" x 24"

Hook this great antique-looking rug with a wide variety of hand-dyed black woolens for the background to create an instant "aged" effect. Choose warm black colors with undertones of browns and green to create an older look instantly!

Hooking the Rug

1. Use marker to draw a 19" x 24" rectangle centered on the foundation fabric.

2. Use pen or pencil to trace the full-size Primitive Floral pattern from the pullout pattern sheet onto the red dot tracer fabric.

3. Use marker to transfer the pattern onto the foundation, centering the design within the drawn rectangle.

4. Cut the wool strips necessary to begin the project.

5. Hook the design in the following order with the suggested wools (or other wool colors of choice):
- center of red flower with gold
- outline same flower center with blue
- outline same flower petals with crisp gold
- flower petals with assorted reds

6. Hook the large leaves, first by outlining them and hooking the veins, then by going back and filling in the body of the leaves.

7. Repeat steps 5 and 6 on the remaining flowers and leaves, using varying colors for the flowers.

8. Hook around each of the shapes with one to two rows of background color.

9. Hook one to two rows of background color around the inside of the drawn rectangle line.

10. Hook the rest of the rug background. Try hooking in various directions or hooking shapes and curves into the background to add more movement.

11. Finish the rug according to the instructions in Chapter 5, choosing one of the binding methods on pages 55-61.

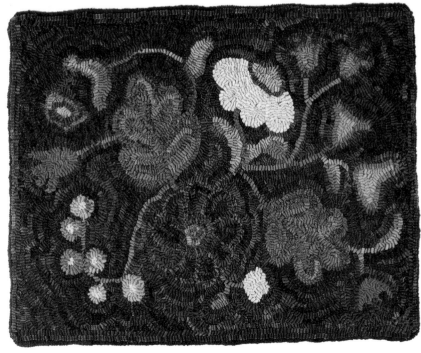

Bouquet of Love

Inspired by my husband who brings flowers frequently and always has lots of love for me and our children, this project combines simple odd-shaped little flowers that burst with colors with hearts for a lovely, meaningful design.

Materials

(Yardage based on 54"-wide fabrics and using #8 cut wool strips.)

18" x 19" foundation fabric

¼-yard butter cream hand-dyed wool (background)

⅛-yard red wool (heart)

⅛-yard purple wool (flowers)

¹⁄₁₆-yard red outline wool (heart and lettering)

¹⁄₁₆-yard gold wool (flower centers)

¹⁄₁₆-yard green wool (stems and leaves)

¼-yard red dot tracer fabric

Fine-point permanent black marker

Bouquet of Love pattern

Planning for this Project

Finished size: 9¼" x 10¾"

The background color used for this rug is the Butter Cream recipe provided on page 40. Here natural-colored wool was over-dyed to achieve the shade shown in the model. A tea-dyed or onionskin-dyed background would also look great.

The purple wool for the flowers worked well with the background color and the red in the rug, but the color was a bit brighter than I normally use. A wonderful muted gold wool in the center of each flower worked to tone the brightness down a bit. These two colors are opposite each other on the color wheel and work well together.

Hooking the Rug

1. Use marker to draw a 9¼" x 10¼" rectangle centered on the foundation fabric.

2. Use pen or pencil to trace the full-size Bouquet of Love pattern from the pullout pattern sheet onto the red dot tracer fabric. Also draw letters in the lower right corner for initials if desired.

3. Use marker to transfer the pattern onto the foundation fabric, centering the design inside the drawn rectangle.

4. Cut the wool strips necessary to begin the project.

5. Hook the design in the following order with the suggested wools (or other wool colors of choice):

- outline of the heart with red
  (Be sure to hook just inside the drawn line.)
- heart with red
- flower centers with gold
- flower "petals" with purple
- stems and leaves with green
- initials with purple (optional)

6. Hook two rows along the outside edge of the rug design with background wool, making sure to hook just inside the drawn pattern line.

7. Hook one to two rows around the outer edges of the flowers and heart with background wool where room permits.

8. Finish filling in the rug background.

9. Finish the rug according to the instructions in Chapter 5, choosing one of the binding methods on pages 55–61.

Saltbox Pillow

Pillows are another great addition to anyone's home. This simple primitive saltbox design hooks up quickly and can add a special spark of color to your décor.

Materials

(Yardage based on 54"-wide wool fabrics and using #8 cut wool strips.)

18" x 19" foundation fabric
⅛-yard assorted green wools (grass and tree leaves)
⅛-yard assorted blue wools (sky background)
8" x 16" red wool (house)
8" x 16" black wool (roof, windows and door)
1" x 16" brown wool (tree trunk)
1" x 16" darker red wool (outlines on house)
⅔-yard wool fabric (backing and pillow top sides)
¼-yard red dot tracer fabric
Fine-point permanent black marker
16 ounces Polyfil stuffing
Rotary cutter or scissors
Rotary mat or ruler
Saltbox Pillow pattern

Planning for this Project

Finished size: 18" x 19"

When deciding what to use for the finished pillows, choose a color of wool fabric that accents the hooked area. Plaids add that extra "homespun" feel. Feel free to substitute 100 percent cotton fabric for the wool as well.

Hooking the Rug

1. Use marker to draw a 9½" x 10½" rectangle centered on the foundation fabric.

2. Use pen or pencil to trace the full-size Saltbox Pillow pattern from the pullout pattern sheet onto the red dot tracer fabric.

3. Use marker to transfer the pattern onto the foundation fabric, centering the design inside the drawn rectangle.

4. Cut wool fabric into strips for the pillow top and backing as follows:
- two 4" x 11" strips
  (top and bottom of pillow top)
- two 4" x 1½" strips
  (right and left sides of pillow top)
- 18½" x 19½" piece (backing)

5. Position the 4" x 11" fabric strips on the top and bottom of the pattern drawn on the foundation fabric. If the wool fabric has a right side and a wrong side, the right side should be facing the pattern and the edges of the strip should extend ½" outside the drawn lines.

6. Stitch ½" from the raw edge of the fabric border, along the drawn line of the pattern, as in Figure 6-11.

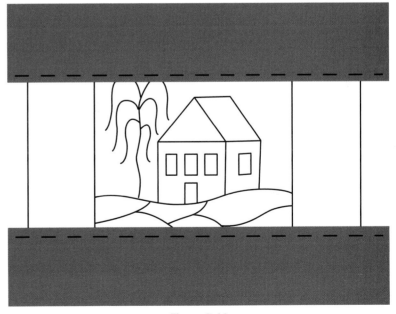

Figure 6-11

7. Use an iron to press the wool fabric pillow borders away from the design.

8. Sew the two side borders of the pillow following the same procedure as in steps 6 and 7 for the look shown in Figure 6-12.

9. Cut the wool strips necessary to begin the project.

10. Hook the design in the following order with the suggested wools (or other wool colors of choice):
- windows and the door with black
- outline of the house corners with darker red
- house with red
- roof with black

11. Hook at least one row along the outside edge of the design with assorted green wools for the grass area and blue wools for the sky area. Be sure to hook right up to the sewn-on fabric borders.

12. Finish hooking the grass in assorted green wools. Vary the greens for a very "patchwork" effect in the rug.

13. Hook the tree trunk with brown and the leaves in green.

14. Finish filling in the sky area with blue wools.

15. Steam the finished hooked piece and allow to dry flat completely.

Figure 6-12

Assembling the Pillow

1. Trim the excess foundation fabric, leaving ½" all around.

2. Pin the 18½" x 19½" wool fabric backing piece to the hooked pillow top with right sides together and matching the raw edges.

3. Stitch around all four sides of the pillow, leaving a 2" to 3" turn-hole.

4. Turn pillow right-side out and stuff.

5. Slipstitch the turn-hole closed.

Vintage Tulips

Traditional folk art-style quilts and the history behind the designs are fascinating.
This design was adapted from an 1800s quilt block. Someday, I'd like to make
a quilt using the deep reds, golds and greens that were popular in the late-1800s
quilts, but for now, I have a great primitive hooked version for my home instead.

Planning for this Project

(Yardage based on 54"-wide wool fabrics and using #8 cut wool strips.)

22" x 25" piece foundation fabric
1 yard primitive black wool (background)
¼-yard assorted green wools (leaves and stems)
12" x 16" piece red wool (flowers)
12" x 16" piece orange wool (flowers)
4" x 16" piece red plaid wool (outline on flowers)
2" x 16" piece orange plaid wool (outline on flowers)
2" x 16" piece gold wool (flowers)
Fine-point permanent black marker
1 yard red dot tracer fabric
22 yards 100% wool yarn or 2¾ yards wool (rug edge binding)
Vintage Tulips pattern

Finished size: 14" × 16½"

Have fun when choosing the colors with this rug; use colors from your wool stash that you love! The flowers can be hooked in a variety of colors to create a beautiful piece for your home. Another great idea is to use a beautiful multicolored spot-dyed piece of wool to really add spark to this piece.

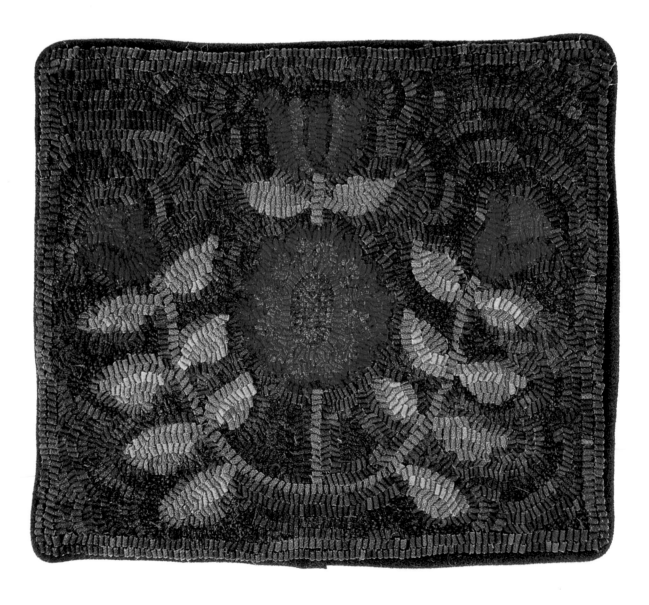

Hooking the Rug

1. Use marker to draw a 14" x 16½" rectangle centered on the foundation fabric.

2. Use pen or pencil to trace the full-size Vintage Tulip pattern from the pullout pattern sheet onto the red dot tracer fabric.

3. Use marker to transfer the pattern onto the foundation fabric, centering the design inside the drawn square.

4. Cut the wool strips necessary to begin the project.

5. Hook the design in the following order with the suggested wools (or other wool colors of choice):

- center oval shape of the large flower with gold plaid
- outline of the middle of the large flower with orange plaid
- middle petals of the large flower with orange
- outline of the large flower with red plaid
- outer petals of the large flower with red
- outline center section of top tulip with red plaid wool
- center section of top tulip with red
- outline of right and left center sections of top tulip with orange plaid
- right and left center sections of top tulip with orange
- outline of outer sections of top tulip with red plaid
- outer sections of top tulip with red
- outline outer sections of two remaining tulips with red plaid
- outer section of two remaining tulips with red
- outline center tops of two remaining tulips with orange plaid
- center tops of two remaining tulips with orange
- stems with green
- leaves with green

6. Hook one to two rows of black background wool around the entire perimeter of the rug, staying just inside the drawn line.

7. Hook one to two rows of background color around the entire design where room permits.

8. Finish filling in the background.

9. Finish the rug according to the instructions in Chapter 5, choosing one of the binding methods on pages 55-61.

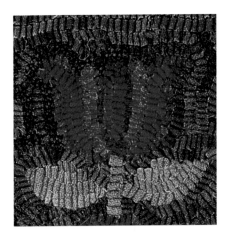

Barn Star

If you share my fascination with barns, you dream of one day moving to the country and owning a whole slew of barns where you and the kids can romp and play. One day while driving through the hills of Kentucky on a camping journey, I noticed the huge number of barns with barn symbols either hanging on the side or painted on the exterior. I knew instantly I wanted to hook one up as a simple reminder to follow my goals of owning a home—and barns—in the country.

Materials

(Yardage based on 54"-wide wool fabrics and using #8 cut wool strips.)

26" square foundation fabric

½-yard butter cream hand-dyed wool (background)

16" x 40" brown herringbone plaid wool (outer border)

¼-yard red wool (star points)

¼-yard blue wool (circles)

⅛-yard gold wool (circle centers)

1 yard red dot tracer fabric

Fine-point permanent black marker

Barn Star pattern

Planning for this Project

Finished size: 18½"-diameter

The background color in this rug is the Butter Cream recipe provided on page 40. Tan houndstooth wool was over-dyed to achieve the shade shown in the model. A tea-dyed or onionskin-dyed background would also look great.

Hooking the Rug

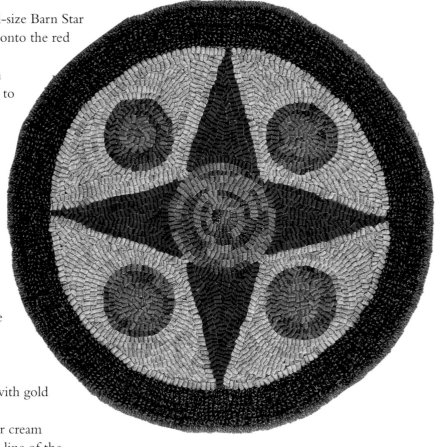

1. Use pen or pencil to trace the full-size Barn Star pattern from the pullout pattern sheet onto the red dot tracer fabric.

2. Use marker to transfer the pattern onto the foundation fabric, taking care to maintain the round shape of the rug.

3. Cut the wool strips necessary to begin the project.

4. Hook the design in the following order with the suggested wools (or other wool colors of choice):

- outline of the center circle of the star, hooking just inside the drawn line with blue and gold alternating
- center circle of the star, following the outline and working toward the center with blue and gold
- outline of the star points with red
- star points with red
- centers of each background circle with gold
- background circles with blue

5. Hook one to two rows with butter cream background wool just inside the drawn line of the inner circle pattern.

6. Finish filling in the background with butter cream.

7. Hook the outer border with the brown herringbone wool.

8. Finish the rug according to the instructions in Chapter 5, choosing one of the binding methods on pages 55-61.

Folk Art Cat

Cats are another common image found often in early rug designs. This special little kitty pattern was designed for my daughter's cat, Miss Ruby. This rug has a great aged, primitive feel that can be achieved by hooking the background in a crazy patch or hit-and-miss design.

Materials

(Yardage based on 54"-wide wool fabrics and using #8 cut wool strips.)

25" x 32" foundation fabric

½-yard assorted black wools (cat)

1⅛ yards assorted colored wools (background)

1" x 16" gold wool (cat eyes)

30 yards wool yarn or ½-yard wool fabric (binding)

1 yard red dot tracer fabric

Fine-point permanent black marker

Folk Art Cat pattern

Planning for this Project

Finished size: 17" x 24"

The background on this rug is called a "crazy patch" or "hit-or-miss" style. When choosing the background wools take care to choose wools that all work well together. If your cat will be hooked in warm antique-looking black wools, be sure to choose warm background wools for the rug. The same holds true if you hook the cat in cool black wools, as you then should choose cool colors for the background, too.

Hooking the Rug

1. Use marker to draw a 17" x 24" rectangle onto the foundation fabric.

2. Use pen or pencil to trace the full-size Folk Art Cat pattern from the pullout pattern sheet onto the red dot tracer fabric. Draw in different shapes and squiggle lines around the cat, as in Figure 6–13, to act as a guide during hooking. Refer to the project photo at left, if needed.

3. Use marker to transfer the pattern onto the foundation fabric, drawing all lines, including the ones drawn in for the background.

4. Cut the wool strips necessary to begin the project.

Figure 6-13

5. Hook the design in the following order with the suggested wools (or other wool colors of choice):

- outline of the cat eyes with gold
- cat eyes with gold
- outline of the cat with assorted blacks
- cat with assorted blacks

6. Hook one to two rows around the cat with the assorted background wools.

7. Hook four straight rows with black, following the entire perimeter of the drawn rectangle.

8. Finish filling in the background with assorted wools in the crazy patch style.

9. Finish the rug according to the instructions in Chapter 5, choosing one of the binding methods on pages 55–61.

Hit-or-Miss Stars

Many wool scraps can be used in this small rug design. This is the perfect size rug to place at the bottom of your stairs or as a table enhancement, as shown in the photo. Hook some of the same fabric you use in the stars into the background so that the stars appear more hidden in the design for a great effect.

Materials

(Yardage based on 54"-wide fabrics and using #8 cut wool strips.)

18" x 28" piece foundation fabric

¼-yard gold wool (stars)

¼-yard black tweed wool (border)

½-yard assorted color wools (background)

22 yards wool yarn or ¼-yard wool (rug edge binding)

½-yard red dot tracer fabric

Fine-point permanent black marker

Hit-or-Miss Stars pattern

Planning for this Project

Finished size: 10" x 20"

Dig into your scrap basket and have fun with this background. I tossed all of my "worms," which is another word for the strips, into a paper grocery bag and set it next to my hooking. When I needed another strip, I went into the bag without looking, pulled out a strip and used it. This is a great way to make a hit-or-miss background.

1. Use marker to draw a 10" x 20" rectangle centered on the foundation fabric and draw a second rectangle 1" inside the first, shown in Figure 6-13 below.

2. Use pen or pencil to trace the full-size Hit-or-Miss Stars pattern from the pullout pattern sheet onto the red dot tracer fabric.

3. Use marker to transfer the pattern onto the foundation fabric, centering the center star first and then adding the right and left stars.

4. Cut the wool strips necessary to begin the project.

5. Hook the outline of the stars with gold wool, staying inside the drawn pattern line.

6. Fill the stars in with gold wool.

7. Hook one row with background wools just inside the innermost drawn rectangle line.

8. Finish filling in the background with the assorted strips.

9. Hook the outer border with black or brown herringbone/tweed wool.

10. Finish the rug according to the instructions in Chapter 5, choosing one of the binding methods on pages 55-61.

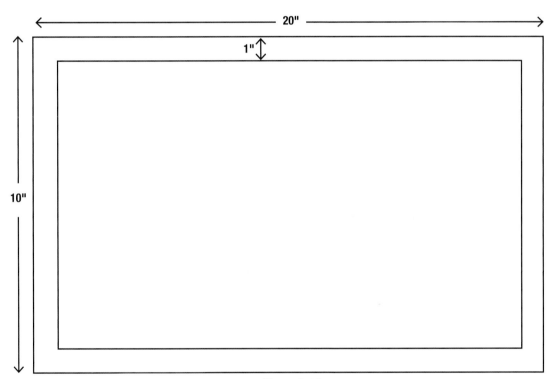

Figure 6-13

Floral Display

This rug was originally designed for display in the fall, but I've just fallen in love with it and now display it all year around. The model shows fall mums in golden and deep orange, rust-colored ones, but you can change the flower colors to suit your own tastes or your décor.

Materials

(Yardage based on 54"-wide wool fabrics and using #8 cut wool strips.)

25" square foundation fabric

¾-yard assorted cream wools (background)

⅛-yard brown wool (vase)

⅛-yard orange wool (flowers)

⅛-yard gold wool (flowers)

⅛-yard green wool (stems and leaves)

3" x 16" piece gold wool (outline flowers)

3" x 16" piece orange wool (outline flowers)

3" x 16" piece blue wool (flower centers)

3" x 16" piece deep red wool (flower centers)

Fine-point permanent black marker

1 yard red dot tracer fabric

25 yards 100% wool yarn (rug edge binding)

Planning for this Project

Finished size: 17" square

This hooked rug is the perfect project for a beginner that has a little more detail. Practice curves and straight lines while putting your knowledge of color to good use. Notice the flowers: Each uses a main color, with its complementary color hooked into the center. The rug is just perfect to use in your home décor.

Hooking the Rug

1. Use marker to draw a 17" square centered on the foundation fabric.

2. Use pen or pencil to trace the full-size Floral Display pattern from the pullout pattern sheet onto the red dot tracer fabric.

3. Use marker to transfer the pattern onto the foundation fabric, centering the design in the drawn square.

4. Cut the wool strips necessary to begin the project.

5. Hook the design in the following order with the suggested wools (or other wool colors of choice):

- outline of the vase with brown, staying just inside the drawn line
- vase with brown
- flower centers with either blue or deep red
- outline of the flowers with either gold or orange
- flowers with either orange or gold
- leaves and stems with green

6. Hook one to two rows around each shape with cream background wools.

7. Hook one to two rows inside the drawn square line with cream background wools.

8. Finish filling in the background. Remember: Hooking in various directions and adding shapes and curves into the background gives the rug more movement.

9. Finish the rug according to the instructions in Chapter 5, choosing one of the binding methods on pages 55–61.

Lovin' America

This design is as American as apple pie. And because it's a simple rug to hook in a smaller size, it is perfect for a beginner. For a variation, instead of hooking the star into this rug, try hooking that entire section blue and then sew on small star-shaped buttons for a wonderful three-dimensional effect.

Materials

(Yardage based on 54"-wide wool fabrics and using #8 cut wool strips.)

18" x 20" piece foundation fabric

16" x 24" piece nutmeg wool (background)

16" x 18" piece oatmeal or cream wool (heart stripes and star)

16" square red wool (heart stripes)

12" x 16" piece blue wool (heart)

Fine-point permanent black marker

½-yard red dot tracer fabric

18 yards wool yarn or 2 yards wool (rug edge binding)

Lovin' America pattern

Planning for this Project

Finished size: 10" x 12"

This rug is an excellent choice for a beginner, as the pattern is easy and quick to hook. Have fun when choosing your wools. Pick several shades of red and blue for a variegated, interesting look. The background on this rug would also look great hooked in Primitive Black; the recipe for this color is provided on page 40.

Hooking the Rug

1. Use marker to draw a 10" x 12" rectangle centered on the foundation fabric and then a second rectangle ¼" inside the first, as shown in Figure 6-14.

2. Draw a third rectangle ¼" inside the second rectangle, as in Figure 6-15.

3. Draw a fourth rectangle ¼" inside the third rectangle, as in Figure 6-16.

4. Use pen or pencil to trace the full-size Lovin' America pattern from the pullout pattern sheet onto the red dot tracer fabric.

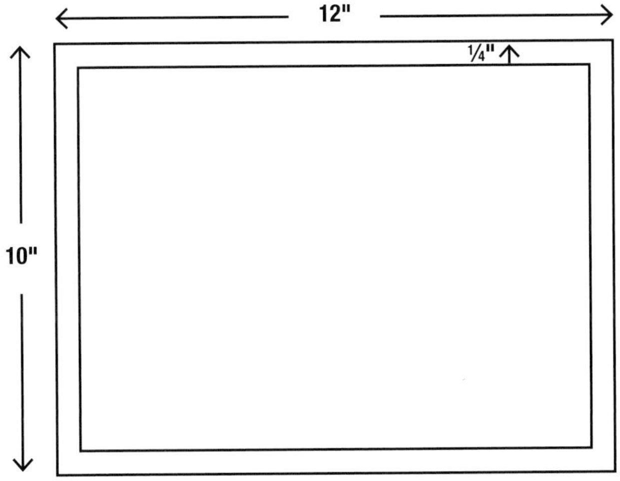

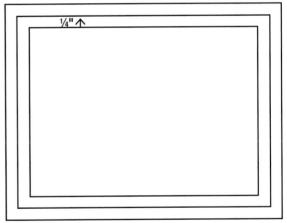

Figure 6-14

Figure 6-15

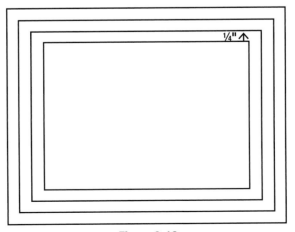

Figure 6-16

5. Use marker to transfer the pattern onto the foundation fabric, centering the design inside the innermost drawn rectangle, as in Figure 6-17.

6. Cut the wool strips necessary to begin the project.

7. Hook the design in the following order with the suggested wools (or other wool colors of choice):

- outline of the star with cream or oatmeal, staying within the drawn pattern lines
- star with cream or oatmeal
- outline upper left flag area with blue
- upper left flag area with blue
- heart stripes, starting at the top of the heart with red for about four rows and then alternating with cream/oatmeal for four rows

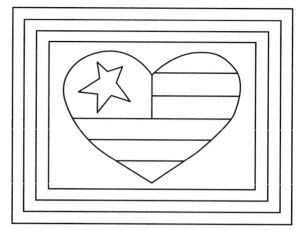

Figure 6-17

8. Hook one row of nutmeg background wool around the heart.

9. Hook one row of nutmeg background wool around the perimeter of the inside rectangle.

10. Finish filling in the background.

11. Hook the first inner border with red.

12. Hook the second inner border with cream/oatmeal.

13. Hook the outer border with blue.

14. Finish the rug according to the instructions in Chapter 5, choosing one of the binding methods on pages 55-61.

Folk Art Bird Cupboard

Have you ever had one of those moments when you see a piece of furniture or a small wooden cabinet and just knew you had a place in your home that was perfect for it? That's what happened when I visited Kindred Spirits in Centerville, Ohio, and saw this handmade cabinet. I knew just what I wanted to hook for the front door and just where it would go in my home. This particular cabinet with its primitive, folk art appeal has a recessed panel on the front to encase your hooked rug. The flowers are hooked using a special piece of hand-dyed wool from Kindred Spirits also.

Materials

(Yardage based on 54"-wide fabrics and using #8 cut wool strips.)

20" x 27" piece foundation fabric

¾-yard butter cream and variety of creams and tans (background)

¼-yard assorted brown wools (bird body)

¼-yard assorted blue wools (bird neck, wing and tail)

16" x 18" piece assorted red wools (bird head and berries)

7" x 16" piece spot-dyed wool (flowers)

2" x 16" piece green wools (stem)

1" x 16" piece mustard wool (beak)

Large hinged cupboard*

Fine-point permanent black marker

1 yard red dot tracer fabric

Clear silicone glue (from local hardware store)

16" x 23" heavy-duty piece cardboard

Folk Art Bird pattern

Used for this project: Large hinged cupboard from Kindred Spirits (Resources, page 128).

Planning for this Project

Finished size: 12" x 18½"

This project makes a nice display piece with extra storage inside. Inspiration for the design struck the minute I purchased the cupboard and by the time I reached home from a six-hour trip, the perfect primitive/folk art bird had come alive in my mind. The rug was drawn out and hooked within two days!

The cupboards come in many different colors and your wools easily can be coordinated to match. With its handy leather closing strip, it's a truly excellent antique reproduction. And if a cupboard does not meet your needs, try either framing the design or finishing it as a rug, according to the instructions in Chapter 5.

Hooking the Rug

1. Use marker to draw a 12" x 18½" rectangle on the foundation fabric. The rectangle measurements are sized so that the drawn pattern will be ¼" smaller on every side than the inside dimensions of the cupboard. This scant ¼" gap is necessary so there is room to fit the rug inside the recessed lid without it puckering up.

Tara's Tip: Whether you purchase a reproduction cupboard from Kindred Spirits for this project (as in the model), be sure to double-check the measurements of the rectangle drawn in step 1 against the measurements of the recessed front door.

2. Use pen or pencil to trace the full-size Folk Art Bird pattern from the pullout pattern sheet onto the red dot tracer fabric.

3. Use marker to transfer the pattern onto the foundation fabric, centering the design inside the drawn rectangle.

4. Cut the wool strips necessary to begin the project.

5. Hook the design in the following order with the suggested wools (or other wool colors of choice):

- outline of main body with assorted browns
- main body with assorted browns
- legs with assorted browns
- outline of wing with assorted blues
- wing with assorted blues
- outline of neck with assorted blues
- neck with assorted blues
- tail feathers with assorted blues
- eye with butter cream
- outline of head with assorted reds
- head with assorted reds
- flowers with spot-dyed wools
- vines with greens

Tara's Tip: Notice how I tried to "highlight" the eye of the bird by using a very dark strip of red wool and then outlining the head area with a darker color, too.

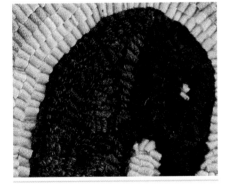

Tara's Tip: Here is a handy tip for making adjustments in step 10. If your finished hooked piece ends up being larger than the recessed area, simply rip out a row of hooking around the outer edges to make the project fit. If your finished hooked piece is too small, add another row of hooking as necessary. If you hook this project on monk's cloth, it will tend to stretch as you hook, which could cause your project to be slightly larger than expected. Keep in mind that if you have a very narrow area around the perimeter of your project after it is hooked and centered in the recessed area of the cabinet, you could always get creative by adding a piece of colored cording around the hooked piece that coordinates with the project to fill in the gaps.

6. Hook one to two rows with butter cream/cream/tan background wools around the bird. Try using the lightest shade of background wool to give the bird a "shadow" or "halo" look and really make it pop out.

7. Hook one or two rows of background around the entire outside border edge, staying inside the drawn line and not on it.

8. Check the rug measurements against the inner recessed part of the cupboard door to ensure it fits.

9. Finish filling in the remaining background.

10. Check again to be sure the rug fits inside the recessed area of the cupboard and make any adjustments if needed.

11. Lay a heavy-duty piece of cardboard down on a hard, flat surface and place the finished rug right-side up on top.

12. Run a line of clear silicone glue around the perimeter directly next to the last row of hooking on the foundation fabric only.

13. Smooth the glue outward on the foundation fabric using your finger. It is important to completely cover the foundation fabric surrounding the last rows of hooking.

14. Allow the project to dry overnight.

Attaching the Cupboard

1. Use a sharp pair of scissors to cut away all excess foundation fabric so that only the outer thread of the foundation fabric remains on the outside edge of the hooking.

2. Wipe the front of the cupboard clean to remove any dust or fibers.

3. Apply a thin line of clear silicone glue around the inside edge of the cupboard door, as well as a small amount to the center. Do not overdo on the glue, as it can seep up through the hooked design if too much is applied.

4. Insert the rug into the top recessed edge of the cupboard and apply pressure. It takes a few minutes before the glue starts to set up, so adjust as needed.

5. Lay a heavy book on top of the rug and cupboard overnight to apply pressure for a good glue seal.

My Flurry Friend

Snowmen are the perfect winter decoration, as they fit in with the holidays but do not have to be taken down until that last flake falls in February or March. My Flurry Friend is an adaptation of another one of my daughter's drawings from kindergarten. Use a couple different shades of blue in the background to create a great wintery scene.

Materials

(Yardage based on 54"-wide wool fabrics and using #8 cut wool strips.)

21" x 25" piece foundation fabric

⅓-yard assorted blue wools (background)

⅓-yard assorted darker blue wools (border)

¼-yard butter cream wool (snowman)

⅛-yard red plaid wool (scarf and border)

2" x 16" piece brown wool (twig arms)

1" x 16" piece orange wool (snowman nose)

Fine-point permanent black marker

½-yard red dot tracer fabric

22 yards 100% wool yarn or 2 yards wool
(rug edge binding)

My Flurry Friend pattern

Planning for this Project

Finished size: 13" x 17"

This is a quick-and-easy project that makes a great last-minute gift, or a beautiful addition to your holiday decorating. Get creative with your wool choices and make your snowman look "briskly" cool by using a shade of off-white wool with "hints" of blue dyed into it. The background would also look great hooked up using a piece of wool that is dyed a cool shade of blue with hints of violet or plum.

Hooking the Rug

1. Use marker to draw a 13" x 17" rectangle centered on the foundation fabric and draw a second rectangle 1½" inside the first.

2. Use pen or pencil to trace the full-size My Flurry Friend pattern from the pullout pattern sheet onto the red dot tracer fabric.

3. Use marker to transfer the pattern onto the foundation fabric, centering the design inside the drawn rectangle.

4. Cut the wool strips necessary to begin the project.

5. Hook the design in the following order with the suggested wools (or other wool colors of choice):

- outline of the scarf with red plaid, starting just inside the drawn lines
- scarf with red plaid
- snowman nose with orange
- twig arms with brown
- outline of the snowman with butter cream, starting just inside the drawn lines
- snowman with butter cream

6. Hook one row with assorted blue background strips around the perimeter, just inside the drawn rectangle.

7. Hook one row in background colors around the snowman body.

8. Finish filling in the background.

9. Hook two rows in the outside border with the darker blue wools.

10. Hook the third row of the border, alternating one strip of darker blue wool with one strip of red plaid.

11. Hook the remaining two rows of the border with darker blue wools.

12. Finish the rug according to the instructions in Chapter 5, choosing one of the binding methods on pages 55–61.

Flag Footstool

These simple wood footstools make the perfect foundation for an Americana piece.
The rug hooks up easily and is great for beginners.

Materials

(Yardage based on 54"-wide fabrics and using #8 cut wool strips.)

17" x 19" piece foundation fabric

16" x 28" piece assorted cream-colored wools (stripes)

16" x 28" piece assorted red wools (stripes)

16" x 18" piece assorted blue wools (upper left flag)

Small cream footstool*

2¼ yards ⅛" blue cording

Fine-point permanent black marker

1 sheet clear template plastic

Ruler

Scissors

Clear silicone glue (from local hardware store)

Tacky glue*

13" x 15" heavy-duty piece cardboard

Heavy-duty hook-and-loop tape (optional)

*Used for this project: Wayne Sims Folkart stool (Resources, page 128) and Aleene's Tacky Glue.

Planning for this Project

Finished size: 8⅝" x 10½"

Have fun while choosing your wools for this flag design. Try an assortment of different shades of creams, reds and blues and watch the design come to life! You could even add a star in the blue area of the rug just for fun. Or look for small star buttons and attach those to your flag for an instant three-dimensional effect.

If you would rather use this piece for a mat instead of attaching it to a footstool, finish the rug according to the directions in Chapter 5, using your preferred method of binding.

Hooking the Rug

1. Use marker to draw an 8⅝" x 10½" rectangle centered on the foundation fabric, using your permanent marker. The rectangle measurements are sized so that the drawn pattern will be ¼" smaller on every side than the top of the footstool. This ¼" gap is necessary so the edges of the rug will not hang off.

Tara's Tip: Whether you purchase a wood footstool from Wayne Sims Folkart for this project (as in the model), be sure to double-check the measurements of the rectangle drawn in step 1 against the measurements of the top flat edge of the stool.

2. Draw a second rectangle ¼" inside the first rectangle, as shown in Figure 6-18. (The space between the two is the border area.)

3. Place the foundation fabric so that the 10½" drawn lines of the rectangle are running horizontally and draw a 4⅜" x 4" rectangle in the upper left corner of the pattern, as in Figure 6-19.

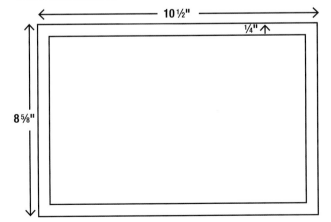

Figure 6-18

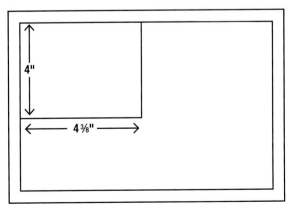

Figure 6-19

4. Draw seven straight lines across the inside rectangle spaced 1" apart for the flag stripes, as in Figure 6-20.

5. Cut the wool strips necessary to begin the project.

6. Hook the design in the following order with the suggested wools (or other wool colors of choice):

- outside ¼" border with blue
- upper left rectangle with assorted blues
- stripes, alternating red for four rows and then cream for four rows

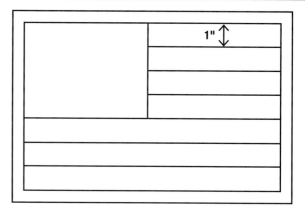

Figure 6-20

Attaching the Stool

1. Wipe the top of the footstool clean to remove any dust or fibers.

2. Lay a heavy-duty piece of cardboard down on a hard, flat surface and place the hooked piece right-side up on top.

3. Run a line of clear silicone glue directly next to the last row of hooking and around the entire perimeter on the foundation fabric only.

4. Smooth the glue outward on the foundation fabric with your finger. It is important to completely cover the foundation fabric surrounding the last row of hooking.

5. Allow the project to dry overnight.

6. Use a sharp pair of scissors to cut away all excess foundation fabric as close to the hooked loops as possible.

7. Apply a thin line of clear silicone glue ½" in from the outside edge of the stool, as well as a small amount to the center.

8. Center the rug over the top of the footstool and apply pressure. It takes a few minutes before the glue starts to set up, so adjust as needed.

9. Lay a heavy book on top of the rug and stool overnight to apply pressure for a good glue seal.

10. Run a thin line of tacky glue along the outside edges of the rug.

11. Lay the cording next to the edges and around the perimeter of the rug, pressing it down into the glue.

12. Trim off excess cording and rub a small amount of glue on the ends to prevent fraying.

13. Optional: To make the rug removable from the footstool so that you can interchange rugs, use heavy-duty hook-and-loop tape on the rug(s) and stool.

Love Never Melts

This design, made with the ever-popular snowman theme, makes a great decoration in front of your tree during the holiday season.

Materials

(Yardage based on 54"-wide wool fabrics and using #8 cut wool strips, unless otherwise noted.)

21" x 27" piece foundation fabric

½-yard blue wool (background)

16" x 25" piece darker blue wool (border)

16" x 28" piece butter cream wool (snowman)

16" square red wool (hatband and border)

10" x 16" piece black wool (eyes and buttons)

6" x 16" piece of each (all in #6 cut):
- red plaid wool (scarf)
- blue plaid wool (scarf)
- gold plaid wool (scarf)

3" x 16" piece orange wool (snowman nose in #6 cut)

Fine-point permanent black marker

½-yard red dot tracer fabric

24 yards 100% wool yarn or 2½ yards wool (rug edge binding)

Love Never Melts pattern

Planning for this Project

Finished size: 12½" x 18½"

The color combinations are endless for this easy-to-hook rug. Hook the scarf in different shades of colors that would go well in your own home. The scarf is also an excellent area to practice using different plaid wools from your collection. For the outer border, try a blue about two shades darker than what was hooked into the background of the rug, as in the model. This makes the snowman really "pop" out at you and lets the borders have more of a subtle effect in the background.

Hooking the Rug

1. Use marker to draw a 12½" x 18½" rectangle centered on the foundation fabric and then a second rectangle 1" inside the first, as shown in Figure 6-21.

2. Use pen or pencil to trace the full-size Love Never Melts pattern from the pullout pattern sheet onto the red dot tracer fabric.

3. Use marker to transfer the pattern onto the foundation fabric, centering the design inside the drawn rectangle and placing the bottom edge of the snowman even with the bottom line of the inside rectangle.

4. Cut the wool strips necessary to begin the project.

5. Hook the design in the following order with the suggested wools (or other wool colors of choice):

- snowman's nose with orange
- snowman's eyes with black
- coal buttons with black
- snowman's scarf with small thin strips in blue plaid, alternating the red and the gold plaids, as shown in the model photo
- outline of the snowman with butter cream
- snowman with butter cream
- wording with one row butter cream
- snowflakes with one row butter cream
- hatband with red
- outline of hat with black
- hat with black

6. Hook one row with blue background strips around the perimeter just inside the innermost drawn rectangle.

7. Hook one row of blue background around the snowman.

8. Finish filling in the background.

9. Hook the border with the darker blue wools.

10. Finish the rug according to the instructions in Chapter 5, choosing one of the binding methods on pages 55-61.

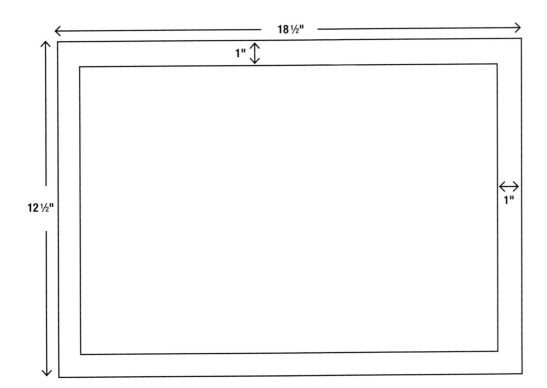

Figure 6-21

Flower-in-Vase Pillow

This little rug design came about when my daughter picked a single flower from my newly planted flowerbeds one year. We placed the flower in a vase that she had painted for me and put it on the kitchen table. When I look at this pillow, I smile and think of how she loves to plant flowers with me—only to pick them not long after!

Materials

(Yardage based on 54"-wide wool fabrics and using #8 cut wool strips.)

15" x 20" piece foundation fabric
15" x 16" piece butter cream or cream wool (background)
15" x 16" piece brown plaid or herringbone wool (vase and border)
15" x 16" piece gold wool (flower and star)
5" x 16" piece red wool (flower)
2" x 16" piece purple plaid wool (flower center)
1½" x 16" piece green wool (stem and leaves)
⅔-yard homespun fabric (outer borders and pillow backing)
¼-yard red dot tracer fabric
Fine-point permanent black marker
Polyfil stuffing
Flower-in-Vase pattern

Planning for this Project

Finished size: 17" x 22"

When deciding what to use for the finished pillow, choose a color of wool fabric that accents the hooked area. Plaids add that extra "homespun" feel. Feel free to substitute 100 percent cotton fabric for the wool as well.

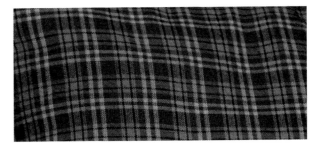

Hooking the Rug

1. Use marker to draw a 7" x 12" rectangle centered on the foundation fabric and then a second rectangle ½" inside the first, as shown in Figure 6-22.

2. Use pen or pencil to trace the full-size Flower-in-Vase pattern from the pullout pattern sheet onto the red dot tracer fabric.

3. Use marker to transfer the pattern onto the foundation fabric, centering the design inside the innermost drawn rectangle.

4. Cut wool fabric into strips for the pillow top and backing as follows:
- two 6" x 8" pieces (top and bottom of pillow top)
- two 6" x 23" pieces
 (right and left sides of pillow top)
- 18" x 23" piece (backing)

5. Position the 6" x 8" fabric strips on the top and bottom of the pattern drawn on the foundation fabric. If the wool fabric has a right side and a wrong side, the right side should be facing the pattern and the edges of the strip should extend ½" outside the drawn lines.

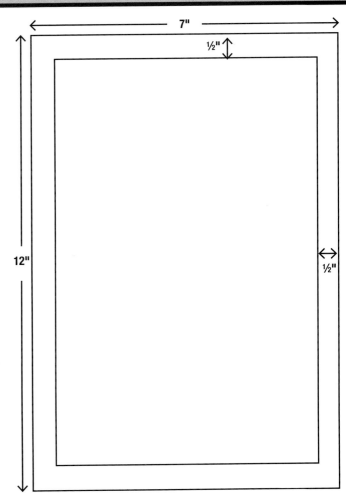

Figure 6-22

6. Stitch ½" from the raw edge of the fabric border, along the drawn line of the pattern, as in Figure 6-23 below left.

7. Use an iron to press the wool fabric pillow borders away from the design.

8. Sew the two side borders of the pillow following the same procedure as in steps 6 and 7 for the look shown below right in Figure 6-24.

9. Cut the wool strips necessary to begin the project.

10. Hook the design in the following order with the suggested wools (or other wool colors of choice):

- outline of the flower with two rows red, starting just inside the drawn line
- second section of the flower with two rows gold
- flower center with purple
- stems with green
- leaves with green
- outline of the vase star with gold
- vase star with gold
- outline of vase with brown plaid/herringbone
- vase with brown plaid/herringbone

11. Hook two rows for the outer border with brown plaid wool. The outermost row needs to be hooked right up next to the homespun fabric, with the second row coming inward on the rug.

12. Hook one to two rows of butter cream or cream background just inside of the outer border.

13. Hook one to two rows background color where possible around the flower and vase design.

14. Finish filling in the background.

15. Steam the finished hooked piece and allow to dry flat completely.

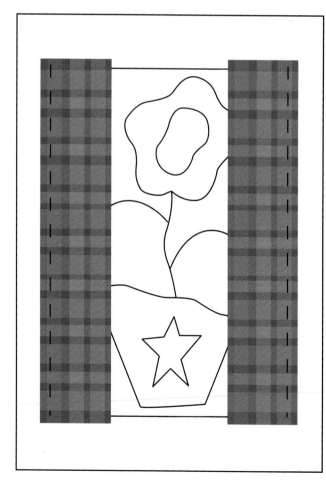

Figure 6-23

Figure 6-24

1. Trim the excess foundation fabric, leaving ½" all around.

2. Pin the 18" x 23" wool fabric backing piece to the hooked pillow top with right sides together and matching the raw edges.

3. Stitch around all four sides of the pillow with a ¼" seam allowance, leaving a 2" to 3" turn-hole.

4. Turn pillow right-side out and fill it with stuffing.

5. Slipstitch the turn-hole closed.

Folk Art Crow

Crows are a favorite primitive bird. This rug was designed after a tour of the Mammouth Caves in Kentucky in which my family was able to see many rather large black bats quietly sleeping. My son was instantly amazed and started yelling, "Mom, the crows, the crows, look!" His enthusiasm stirred the bats up a little too much for my liking—and that of everyone else in our tour group! I get tickled every time I look at this rug, thinking about my 6-year-old's excitement with the "crows."

Materials

(Yardage based on 54"-wide wool fabrics and using #8 cut wool strips.)

21" x 28" piece foundation fabric

16" x 25" piece assorted black or deep purple wool (crow)

¾-yard assorted cream and tan wool (background)

Fine-point permanent black marker

1 yard red dot tracer fabric

30 yards 100% wool yarn or 2¾ yards wool
(rug edge binding)

Folk Art Crow pattern

Planning for this Project

Finished size: 13" x 19½"

When deciding on the "perfect" color to hook the crow, remember this is a primitive project and crows do not always have to be black. Use a piece of wool or several that are dyed a deep, dark eggplant shade. Or better yet, use bits and pieces of a primitive black wool and strips of dark navy blue and deep purple all together for an amazing finished crow.

Hooking the Rug

1. Use marker to draw a 13" x 19½" rectangle centered on the foundation fabric.

2. Use pen or pencil to trace the full-size Folk Art Crow pattern from the pullout pattern sheet onto the red dot tracer fabric.

3. Use marker to transfer the pattern onto the foundation fabric, centering the design inside the drawn rectangle and placing the bottom edge of the crow even with the drawn line of the inside rectangle.

4. Cut the wool strips necessary to begin the project.

5. Hook the outline of the crow with black or purple, starting just inside the drawn lines.

6. Fill in the crow with black or purple, moving row-by-row from the outline inward.

7. Hook one to two rows of cream/tan background wool around the crow.

8. Hook one to two rows of background color around the outside edges.

9. Finish filling in the background.

10. Finish the rug according to the instructions in Chapter 5, choosing one of the binding methods on pages 55–61.

Folk Heart Pins

Small heart-shaped pins or a special little trinket box are a perfect gift to give someone to let them know you care for them. These pins hook up quickly and provide a great outlet for using up a few remnants of wool.

Materials

(Yardage based on 54"-wide wool fabrics and using #8 cut wool strips.)

12" square foundation fabric (both hearts will fit)

4" x 16" piece red wool (hearts)

2" x 16" piece cream/tan wool (background)

2" x 16" piece light blue wool (background)

6" square wool or craft felt (pin backing)

Fine-point permanent black marker

2 pin backs

Clear silicone glue (from local hardware store)

Cool-melt glue gun and glue sticks

5" x 6" heavy-duty piece cardboard

Ruler

Scissors

Heart Pin pattern

Planning for this Project

Finished size: 2¼" x 2¾"

These small pins are the quickest and most fun pieces to hook up! Hook them in an array of colors to match your outfits or give them as unique gifts! These are a great way to use up leftover scraps of fabric.

Hooking the Rug

These instructions are for one pin only. If you plan to make a second with the remaining foundation fabric, repeat the instructions for the second.

1. Use marker to draw a 2¼" x 2¾" rectangle on the foundation fabric.

2. Use pen or pencil to trace the full-size Heart Pin pattern from the pullout pattern sheet onto the red dot tracer fabric.

3. Use marker to transfer the pattern onto the foundation fabric, centering the heart inside the drawn rectangle.

4. Cut the wool strips necessary to begin the project.

5. Hook the heart with red, starting inside the drawn lines.

6. Hook the background with cream or blue, beginning with one row just inside the drawn line of the rectangle and filling in the remainder.

7. Lay a heavy-duty piece of cardboard down on a hard, flat surface and place the hooked piece right-side up on top.

8. Run a line of clear silicone glue directly next to the last row of hooking and around the entire perimeter on the foundation fabric only.

9. Smooth the glue outward on the foundation fabric with your finger. It is important to completely cover the foundation fabric surrounding the last row of hooking.

10. Allow the project to dry overnight.

Assembling the Pin

1. Use a sharp pair of scissors to cut away all excess foundation fabric as close to the hooked loops as possible.

2. Measure the finished size of the pin from the back and cut a piece of craft felt or wool to this measurement.

3. Hand-stitch pin back in place on the right side of the felt/wool.

4. Hot glue felt/wool to the back of the hooked piece with pin side facing out.

Crazy Star

This rug was designed to use up some leftover scraps of wool and at the same time, create something simple enough for the beginner yet still fun for a more seasoned hooker. This size rug is perfect for an end table, as an accent piece for your bathroom countertop or as a giant-sized coaster or trivet.

Materials

(Yardage based on 54"-wide wool fabrics and using #8 cut wool strips.)

18" square foundation fabric
15" x 16" piece assorted colors wool (star)
16" x 26" piece black wool (background)
Fine-point permanent black marker
½-yard red dot tracer fabric
36 yards 100% wool yarn or 2 yards wool (rug edge binding)
Crazy Star pattern

Planning for this Project

Finished size: 10" square

This rug is excellent for a beginner and yet more seasoned hookers will not be bored! Remember to choose a variety of colors to hook your star to add that "eye-candy" appeal. This rug is a great way to use leftover scraps of wool from your collection.

Hooking the Rug

1. Use marker to draw a 10" square centered on the foundation fabric.

2. Use pen or pencil to trace the full-size Crazy Star pattern from the pullout pattern sheet onto the red dot tracer fabric.

3. Use marker to transfer the pattern onto the foundation, centering the design inside the drawn square.

4. Cut the wool strips necessary to begin the project.

5. Hook the outline of the star with assorted colors, starting just inside the drawn lines.

6. Hook the remainder of the star with assorted colors row–by–row, moving inward from the outline.

7. Hook one row of black background wool around the entire perimeter, just inside the drawn 10" square.

8. Hook one row of background wool around the star shape.

9. Finish filling in the background.

10. Finish the rug according to the instructions in Chapter 5, choosing one of the binding methods on pages 55-61.

American Crow

What is more reminiscent of summer, than a nice slice of juicy watermelon?
In this rug I wanted reminders of some of my favorite summertime memories
when I was a child. Buttons added throughout this design add a great three-
dimensional effect to the finished rug.

Materials

(Yardage based on 54"-wide wool fabrics and using #8 cut wool strips.)

24" x 28" piece foundation fabric

¾-yard assorted muted nutmeg wool (background)

¼-yard assorted brown tweed wool (border)

¼-yard faded light red wool (watermelon)

¼-yard olive green wool (watermelon)

⅛-yard deep red wool (stripes in flag)

⅛-yard butter cream wool (stripes in flag)

8" x 16" faded black wool (crow)

4" x 16" piece blue wool (flag)

1" x 16" piece brown wool (flag)

Fine-point permanent black marker

3 ⅜" star buttons (flag)

12 to 16 round black buttons (⅜" to ½") (watermelon seeds)

¼" clear or white button (crow eye)

¾-yard red dot tracer fabric

36 yards 100% wool yarn or 2 yards wool (rug edge binding)

Thread to match buttons

American Crow pattern

Planning for This Rug

Finished Size: 15½" x 20"

Get creative when planning for this rug and use a deeply mottled piece of wool for the watermelon. Such a wool choice will add extra depth.

Hooking the Rug

1. Use marker to draw a 15½" x 20" rectangle centered on the foundation fabric, a second rectangle 1" inside the first and a third ½" inside the second.

2. Use pen or pencil to trace the full-size American Crow pattern from the pullout pattern sheet onto the red dot tracer fabric.

3. Use marker to transfer the pattern onto the foundation fabric, centering the design inside the drawn rectangle.

4. Cut the wool strips necessary to begin the project.

5. Hook the design in the following order with the suggested wools (or other wool colors of choice):
- crow with faded black
- flag stem with brown
- remaining flag area with blue for the upper left area of the flag, then alternating deep red wool and butter cream wool for the strips
- watermelon with faded light red wool
- brine on watermelon with butter cream wool
- outside of watermelon with olive green wool

6. Hook one row with muted nutmeg background strips around the perimeter, just inside the drawn rectangle.

7. Hook one row in background colors around the crow, flag and watermelon.

8. Finish filling in the background.

9. Hook one row of olive green as the second border.

10. Hook the remaining outer border using brown tweed wool.

11. Finish the rug according to the instructions in Chapter 5, choosing one of the binding methods on pages 55-61.

12. Hand-stitch the ¼" button into place for crow eye.

13. Hand-stitch the three small star buttons onto the blue area of the flag.

14. Hand-stitch black buttons randomly on watermelon.

Resources

Association of Traditional Hooking Artists (ATHA)
1360 Newman Ave.
Seekonk, MA 02771
(508) 399-8230
Association.

Amherst Antiques & Folk Art
Sally Van-Nuys Brown
141 Woodhill Drive
Amherst, OH 44001
(440) 984-3486
sally@amherst-antiques-folkartl.com
www.amherst-antiques-folkart.com
Hand-drawn patterns.

Blackberry Primitives
1944 High St.
Lincoln, NE 68502
(402) 421-1361
(402) 423-8464
www.blackberryprimitives.com
Hand- and mill-dyed wools in
textures, plaids, tweeds, etc. Send $5
for swatches.

Crow Hill Primitives
4 Westvale Road
Kennebunkport, ME 04046
www.crowhillprimitives.com
Hand-drawn patterns.

Emma Lou's Hooked Rugs
Emma Lou Lais
8643 Hiawatha Road
Kansas City, MO 64114
(816) 444-1777
Hand-drawn patterns.

Harry M. Fraser Company
P.O. Box 939
Stoneville, NC 27048
(336) 573-9830
www.fraserrugs.com
Fraser and Bliss cutting machines.

Kindred Spirits
115 Colonial Lane
Kettering, OH 45429
www.kindredspiritsdesigns.com
Hand-dyed wools, Folk Art Bird
cupboard, rug patterns by a variety
of designers, Meno Trigger grip
hooks and the Turtle Creek rug-
hooking frames.

KP Books
700 E. State St.
Iola, WI 54990
(800) 258-0929
www.krause.com
Books. Call for a free catalog.

Mandy's Wool Shed
24 W. Wind Road
West Gardiner, ME 04345
(207) 582-5059
Woolens.

Mary Flanagan Woolens
470 County Road M
Pickett, WI 54964
Mfwoolens@aol.com
Woolens. Send $5 for swatches.

Mennonite Historical Library Goshen College
1700 S. Main St.
Goshen, IN 46526
Tel: (574) 535-7418
Fax: (574) 535-7438
e-mail: mhl@goshen.edu
Historical rugs.

Primitive Spirit
445 W. 19th Ave.
Eugene, OR 97401
(541) 344-4316
Hand-drawn patterns.

Primitive Wool Creek
3713 Flowermeadow St.
Joliet, IL 60431
(815) 725-6802
www.primitivewoolcreek.com
info@primitivewoolcreek.com
Hand-dyed wools, Rigby Cloth
Stripping Machine, foundation
fabric, hooks, frames, patterns and
kits. Send $5 for full-color catalog.

Rigby Precision Products
P.O. Box 158
Bridgton, ME 04009
(207) 647-5679
Wool strip cutters.

Rug Hooking Magazine
1300 Market Street, Suite 202
Lemoyne, PA 17043
(800) 233-9055
Magazine.

The Dorr Mill Store
P.O. Box 88
Guild, NH 03754
(800) 846-3677
www.dorrmillstore.com
dorrmillstore@sugar-river.net
Wools, color palettes, patterns, kits,
many brands of rug hooks, cutters
and frames.

The Needle Nook
100 E. Main St.
East Ligonier, PA 15658
(724) 238-7874
ndlnook@aol.com
Gold Needles and
Paternayan yarn.

The Potted Pear
7045 Pinemill Drive
West Chester, OH 45069
(513) 759-5301
thepottedpear@fuse.net
Hand-drawn patterns.

The Red Saltbox
Wendy Miller
204 S. Third St.
Miamisburg, OH 45342
www.theredsaltbox.com
wendy@theredsaltbox.com
Hand-drawn patterns.

The Wool Street Journal
312 N. Custer
Colorado Springs, CO 80903
(888) RUG-LOOP
Magazine.

The Wool Studio
706 Brownsville Road
Sinking Spring, PA 19608
www.thewoolstudio.com
rebecca@thewoolstudio.com
Woolens. Send $3 for swatches.

Townsend Industries, Inc.
P.O. Box 97
Altoona, IA 50009
(877) 868-3544
Townsend Cutter machine.

Wayne Sims Folkart
P.O. Box 1092
Talladega, AL 35161
(256) 362-8562
WayneSims@aol.com
Footstools (used in Penny Footstool
and Flag Footstool designs) and
other wooden items used in the
following designs: Folk Hearts,
Sheep Box and Love Box.

W. Cushing & Company
P.O. Box 351
Kennebunkport, ME 04046
(800) 626-7847
www.cushing.com
W. Cushing's Acid Dyes for wool
dyeing and all necessary rug
hooking supplies, plus stripper or
cutter machines.

Woolley Fox, LLC
Barbara Carroll
132 Woolley Fox Lane
Ligonier, PA 15658
(724) 238-3004
www.woolleyfox.com
Hand-drawn patterns.

Woolrich
2 Mill St.
Woolrich, PA 17779
(877) 512-7305
(ask for operator #256)
rughooking @woolrich.com
Woolens.